DISEASES & DISORDERS

Radiation Sickness

Toney Allman

LUCENT BOOKS
A part of Gale, Cengage Learning

GALE
CENGAGE Learning·

Detroit • New York • San Francisco • New Haven, Conn • Waterville, Maine • London

© 2013 Gale, Cengage Learning

LIBRARY OF CONGRESS CATALOGING-IN-PUBLICATION DATA

Allman, Toney.
  Radiation sickness / by Toney Allman.
      pages cm. -- (Diseases & disorders)
  Includes bibliographical references and index.
  ISBN 978-1-4205-0900-7 (hardcover)
  1. Radiation injuries. I. Title.
  RC93.A45 2013
  362.1969'897--dc23
                                                    2012033855

Lucent Books
27500 Drake Rd.
Farmington Hills, MI 48331

ISBN-13: 978-1-4205-0900-7
ISBN-10: 1-4205-0900-4

Printed in the United States of America
1 2 3 4 5 6 7 16 15 14 13 12

Table of Contents

"The Most Difficult Puzzles Ever Devised"

Charles Best, one of the pioneers in the search for a cure for diabetes, once explained what it is about medical research that intrigued him so. "It's not just the gratification of knowing one is helping people," he confided, "although that probably is a more heroic and selfless motivation. Those feelings may enter in, but truly, what I find best is the feeling of going toe to toe with nature, of trying to solve the most difficult puzzles ever devised. The answers are there somewhere, those keys that will solve the puzzle and make the patient well. But how will those keys be found?"

Since the dawn of civilization, nothing has so puzzled people—and often frightened them, as well—as the onset of illness in a body or mind that had seemed healthy before. A seizure, the inability of a heart to pump, the sudden deterioration of muscle tone in a small child—being unable to reverse such conditions or even to understand why they occur was unspeakably frustrating to healers. Even before there were names for such conditions, even before they were understood at all, each was a reminder of how complex the human body was, and how vulnerable.

While our grappling with understanding diseases has been frustrating at times, it has also provided some of humankind's most heroic accomplishments. Alexander Fleming's accidental discovery in 1928 of a mold that could be turned into penicillin has resulted in the saving of untold millions of lives. The isolation of the enzyme insulin has reversed what was once a death sentence for anyone with diabetes. There have been great strides in combating conditions for which there is not yet a cure, too. Medicines can help AIDS patients live longer, diagnostic tools such as mammography and ultrasounds can help doctors find tumors while they are treatable, and laser surgery techniques have made the most intricate, minute operations routine.

This "toe-to-toe" competition with diseases and disorders is even more remarkable when seen in a historical continuum. An astonishing amount of progress has been made in a very short time. Just two hundred years ago, the existence of germs as a cause of some diseases was unknown. In fact, it was less than 150 years ago that a British surgeon named Joseph Lister had difficulty persuading his fellow doctors that washing their hands before delivering a baby might increase the chances of a healthy delivery (especially if they had just attended to a diseased patient)!

Each book in Lucent's Diseases and Disorders series explores a disease or disorder and the knowledge that has been accumulated (or discarded) by doctors through the years. Each book also examines the tools used for pinpointing a diagnosis, as well as the various means that are used to treat or cure a disease. Finally, new ideas are presented—techniques or medicines that may be on the horizon.

Frustration and disappointment are still part of medicine, for not every disease or condition can be cured or prevented. But the limitations of knowledge are being pushed outward constantly; the "most difficult puzzles ever devised" are finding challengers every day.

The Relevance of Radiation Sickness Today

Radiation sickness is a serious, often fatal illness caused by exposure to a high amount of radiation from nuclear material. The nuclear age was born when scientists in the United States invented the atomic bomb during World War II (1939–45), and radiation sickness affected thousands of people when the United States dropped two bombs on cities in Japan. Except for that act of war, radiation events have been accidental and extremely rare. Between 1944 and 2000, 417 nuclear accidents have caused radiation injury to about 3,000 humans, leading to just 127 deaths. The likelihood of getting radiation sickness may seem inconsequential in the world today, but most medical, scientific, and governmental defense experts believe that the risk of radiation sickness remains very real. They are concerned that a nuclear event such as a power plant accident or the use of a nuclear weapon could take place, which would threaten a large number of people with radiation sickness.

Nuclear Material Everywhere
The use of nuclear energy for power, medicine, and military defense has become more and more common throughout the

world since the dawn of the atomic age. Two Indian medical researchers, Amit Bhasin and Aparna Ahuja, explain, "Nuclear power provides about 6% of the world's energy and 13–14% of the world's electricity."[1] In the United States 104 nuclear reactors generate nearly 20 percent of the country's electricity. According to the Nuclear Energy Institute (NEI), as of 2012, 436 nuclear power plants generate electricity in thirty different

The nuclear age was born when the United States invented the atomic bomb and dropped it on Japan in August 1945. Radiation sickness affected tens of thousands of Japanese afterward.

countries around the world. Nuclear energy is clean energy, meaning it is emission free. The NEI estimates that without nuclear power plants, emissions of carbon dioxide into the atmosphere in the United States would increase by more than 50 percent. Nevertheless, some environmental organizations such as Greenpeace point out that nuclear power leads to other toxic problems such as nuclear waste dumps and the release of radioactive gases into the air in some parts of the world. Nuclear power plants may mean more nuclear material threatening the well-being of the environment and the world's people.

Radioactive material is also used in many medical settings, though the risk of radiation sickness as a result of these processes is exceedingly small. Doctors and hospitals depend on radioactive devices for diagnosing and treating many disorders and diseases. This is called nuclear medicine, and it involves the use of small amounts of radioactive substances. Some of the modern techniques for examining the inside of the human body—called imaging tests—require that the patient swallow, inhale, or be injected with radioactive material. Medical professionals may diagnose problems safely and noninvasively with, for example, positron-emission tomography (PET) to find cancers and identify tumors. The radioactive material accumulates in the area of the body with the most chemical activity. Since even small tumors have high chemical activity, a PET scan can diagnose the cancer accurately. Heart disease and problems with the brain and nerves may also cause heightened chemical activity, so scans of these areas can diagnose diseases, too. Other nuclear imaging tests are used to scan bones to diagnose bone diseases or to analyze the functioning of some internal organs. Doctors may also use radioactive substances to treat cancerous tumors because radioactive substances can damage and kill body cells. In one form of cancer treatment, for example, radioactive wires are placed around a tumor to kill cancer cells while not coming near or harming normal body cells. Today nuclear medicine is of great benefit for early diagnosis and disease treatment in hospitals around the world.

In the modern world radioactive material is also used in the form of weapons. Military stockpiles of nuclear warheads present another possible source of radiation threat. Although nuclear nations such as the United States and Russia have worked to reduce the number of nuclear warheads and to discourage more nations from building their own nuclear weapons, these nonproliferation efforts have not been completely successful. According to the Federation of American Scientists, there are more than nineteen thousand nuclear warheads in the world. An accident or security breach with any of these radioactive sources could lead to a medical emergency in which doctors would have to know how to handle radiation sickness.

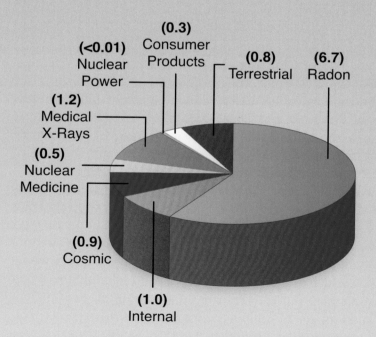

Sources of Radiation Around Us

(0.3) Consumer Products

(<0.01) Nuclear Power

(0.8) Terrestrial

(6.7) Radon

(1.2) Medical X-Rays

(0.5) Nuclear Medicine

(0.9) Cosmic

(1.0) Internal

Total is 11.4 times the amount of radiation emitted by the human body.

Taken from: National Council on Radiation Protection and Measurements. www.ncrponline.org.

Because nuclear material is so prevalent, even if the world stopped using nuclear power plants or nuclear medicine, people might not be free from the threat of radiation sickness. Nuclear terrorism expert and Harvard University professor Graham Allison worries about "dirty bombs" and even the possibility of a terrorist attack with a nuclear bomb. A dirty bomb is a regular bomb or a simple piece of dynamite that contains radioactive waste or other radioactive materials. Because radioactive substances are very common today, an extremist organization might easily acquire radioactive material and combine it with a conventional bomb in order to attack a city. The radiation from such a device would contaminate people in the immediate area. A nuclear bomb would cause devastating destruction and radiation poisoning in a wider geographical area. Allison says that many nuclear bombs in the world could get into the wrong hands. He concludes, "I would not say it's inevitable that there will be a nuclear terror act. . . . But I would say it is highly likely."[2] Many radiation researchers agree with Allison and are, therefore, strongly motivated to understand all they can about radiation sickness and how to treat it.

From the Past to the Future

The effects of radiation are understood largely from just a few historical incidents, but those occasional events have helped to educate the world about the possible effects of a dangerous nuclear incident. They have also driven the research of modern medical experts who do not want to be as helpless as doctors were in the past when they tried to treat and support victims of radiation sickness. Governments also consider the risk of a nuclear disaster and use the lessons of the past to prepare for a future that may include a radiation emergency. In such an emergency the worst and most life-threatening scenario would be one in which people received such high radiation doses that they developed radiation sickness. In the uncertain environment of the modern world, understanding radiation sickness is a matter of importance because it is a matter of saving lives.

CHAPTER ONE

What Is Radiation?

Radiation is energy that originates from a specific source and travels through space. This energy may move in waves or as streams of particles. Many kinds of radiation exist, from many different sources, and people are exposed to radiation every day. Most of this radiation is not harmful, but some kinds of radiation are dangerous and destructive to living things.

The Difference Between Ionizing and Nonionizing Radiation

Different kinds of radiation come from a variety of sources, both natural and human made. The Health Physics Society, an organization of scientific professionals, explains, "When someone mentions the word radiation, we might think of the big mushroom cloud from a nuclear weapon explosion, the microwaves in our microwave oven, how our cell phones work, getting a suntan in a tanning salon, having a chest x ray, or nuclear power plants."[3] All of these are examples of sources of radiation, but they represent different kinds of radiation. The two major categories of radiation are nonionizing radiation and ionizing radiation. Nonionizing radiation is low in energy and comes from such sources as radio and television waves, microwaves, laser lights, cell phones, radar, and sunlight. These waves of energy are rarely dangerous, although too much ultraviolet light from the sun, for example, can cause skin burns or skin cancer. On the electromagnetic spectrum, which is a scale of the range of all the different waves of radiation from lowest

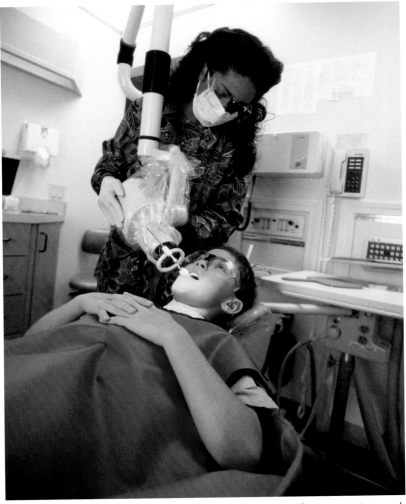

X-rays are an example of ionizing radiation. Dental X-rays, pictured, are a common diagnostic tool used by dentists.

to highest energy, nonionizing radiation is lowest in energy and speed of travel through space. The lower the energy is, the lower the strength and the slower the speed of the radiation. Thus, lower-energy radiation is less harmful to living things than is high-energy radiation.

On the electromagnetic spectrum, ionizing radiation is at the very top of the scale. Ionizing radiation may be in the form of waves or particles, but on the electromagnetic scale, the radiation waves of the highest energy—and the fastest and the strongest—are called gamma rays and X-rays. Sources of natural electromagnetic ionizing radiation include cosmic radiation bombarding the earth from outer space, and elements in the earth itself, such as in rocks, soil, or water. Another source of ionizing radiation to which humans are regularly exposed is medical radiation, such as from X-ray machines. The ionizing radiation from these machines is of such high energy that it penetrates body tissues and gives doctors a picture of what lies under the skin.

Atoms

Ionizing radiation, whether it is in the form of waves like X-rays and gamma rays or in streams of particles, has such high energy that it causes changes in the very atoms of the objects or living things that it penetrates. In order to understand what ionizing radiation is, how it works, why it is called "ionizing," and how it affects people and things, it is necessary to understand something about the atoms that make up all matter. Atoms are made up of a nucleus in the center that consists of protons and neutrons plus electrons that orbit around the nucleus. Neutrons, protons, and electrons are called subatomic particles. Electrons and protons are electrically charged and attract each other. Protons have a positive charge, while electrons are negatively charged. Neutrons are neutral—they have no charge but function to bind protons together in the nucleus. The attraction between the negatively charged electrons and the positively charged protons holds the whole atom together. The number of protons and neutrons present in an atom determines what element the atom is. For example, the element hydrogen has one proton and no neutrons. (A neutron is unnecessary for hydrogen because with just one proton, there is nothing to bind together.) The element aluminum, on the other hand, has thirteen protons and fourteen neutrons. That number of protons in its nucleus is what makes it aluminum or an isotope of aluminum.

The atoms of many elements come in different forms that have different numbers of neutrons in their nuclei. These different forms are called isotopes. A rare isotope of hydrogen, for example, called deuterium, has one proton and one neutron in its nucleus. The atom still stays together and is still stable and balanced in charge, but it is different enough to have slightly different behaviors. For instance, deuterium can be toxic to people.

Unstable Atoms and Ionizing Radiation

Most atoms are stable, but the atoms in the isotopes of nine natural elements and some human-made elements are not. The atoms of these elements have an unbalanced ratio of protons and neutrons in their nuclei. This means that the unbalanced, unstable atoms have too much energy, weight, or both, and something has to change. Explains the Health Physics Society, "Unstable atoms want to be stable atoms so they get rid of some of that energy or weight (or both) to try to be stable. The energy or weight emitted is ionizing radiation."[4] The unstable atom tries to become stable by changing the number of subatomic particles in its nucleus. It may, for instance, convert neutrons to protons and protons to electrons, or it may eject an alpha particle (two neutrons and two protons) from the nucleus. This process of emitting subatomic particles or energy (as electromagnetic waves) is called radioactive decay. The resulting radiation emitted from the atom travels through space and may interact with any matter it meets. It is called ionizing because when the waves or particles encounter other atoms (including those that make up people), it may knock out electrons in those atoms and make them electrically unbalanced. An atom that is positively or negatively charged is called an ion. So ionizing radiation is radiation that can create ions in other atoms.

Sources of Ionizing Radiation

Ionizing radiation may come from natural, unstable, radioactive elements such as uranium. It can also be created artificially by people for energy, medical, or military use. In order to develop

Discovering Radiation

In 1895 Wilhelm Roentgen was studying electric currents when he discovered X-rays. He named them "X-rays" because where they came from and what they were made of was unknown. Then in 1896 Antoine-Henri Becquerel discovered another unknown "ray." In a dark place, Becquerel exposed photographic plates (somewhat like photographic film) to a lump of rock salt that contained uranium. He knew that uranium salts glow when exposed to light, but he did not know that they glowed without light. The photographic plates fogged up from exposure to the uranium. Becquerel had proved that the glow or fogging came from something that the uranium was emitting.

Later in 1896, Marie Curie and her husband, Pierre, decided to study these "Becquerel rays." The Curies spent years investigating uranium and were the first to discover that the rays were energy from the atoms of some elements. They discovered that the element thorium emitted rays, too. By 1898 they discovered two other ray-emitting elements—polonium and radium. Marie coined the word *radioactivity* to describe the energy emissions. Pierre died in an accident in 1906. Marie lived until 1934, when she died of a blood disease caused by years of chronic exposure to radiation from her experiments.

Antoine-Henri Becquerel stands with his experiment that proved uranium salts emitted radioactive energy.

nuclear bombs, for instance, scientists have learned how to shoot neutrons at the unstable atoms of uranium or the human-made element plutonium, thus splitting the nuclei of the atoms and releasing large amounts of energy and radioactivity. This process of splitting nuclei is called fission. Plutonium is so unstable and radioactive that a large enough amount, assembled in one place, will eject neutrons in a quantity that causes a chain reaction of fission among its atoms and will trigger a nuclear explosion. All the subatomic particles in the atom are emitted as energy when the atom splits apart. Scientists use the fission of unstable atoms to create nuclear reactions that release energy. In a controlled way this human-made kind of nuclear radiation is used to produce energy in nuclear power plants in a process called enrichment, or medically as radiation therapy for cancer or in some medical tests. Whether the source of radiation is natural or human-made, nuclear radiation usually produces four major types of ionizing radiation, each with different speeds and strengths.

Types of Ionizing Radiation

The four main types of nuclear radiation are alpha particles, beta particles, gamma rays, and neutron particles. Each type can cause varying degrees of damage to any atoms that are encountered. Alpha particles (two neutrons and two protons) are heavy, slow-moving ionizing radiation. They travel about one-twentieth of the speed of light, which is 186,282 miles per second (299,792km per second). They may be produced naturally or in nuclear reactions. Alpha particles cannot travel very far through space nor pass through matter that is very thick. Instead, when they strike matter they slow down and stop or are absorbed easily by atoms they contact. They can be stopped by less than 1 inch (1cm–2cm) of air or by a piece of paper or a layer of human skin.

Beta particles are electrons emitted by an atom. They are much smaller and lighter than alpha particles and have more energy and more penetrating power. Beta particles can travel through the air about one hundred times farther than alpha

The image shows alpha particles from a radioactive source. Alpha and beta particles, gamma rays, and neutron particles are the four main types of nuclear radiation.

particles. They may travel in air as far as 6 feet (2m) before they slow down and are absorbed. Beta particles cannot penetrate past a layer of clothing or more than 1 inch (1cm–2.54cm) of plastic. Beta particles can result from natural radioactive decay or from human-made nuclear reactions.

Gamma rays are high-energy waves that travel at the speed of light. They are almost the same as X-rays in their penetrating power. Both can travel easily through air and other matter because they are not actual particles—with mass and weight, which slows or prevents the penetration of solid materials, like layers of skin—but waves of energy. Gamma waves have more energy and strength than X-rays, however. They come from the nucleus and are a form of nuclear radiation. (X-rays come from electrons.) Gamma rays are very penetrating and can only be slowed and blocked by heavy materials such as several feet of lead or concrete. Gamma rays also can be emitted because of radioactive decay or from human-made nuclear reactions. Some common sources of human-made gamma radiation are the isotopes of the elements iodine and caesium that are used in medicine.

Neutron particles are neutrons usually released through the process of nuclear fission and in nuclear reactors. They are extremely high-speed, high-energy, penetrating ionizing radiation. The U.S. Nuclear Regulatory Commission says, "Because of their exceptional ability to penetrate other materials, neutrons can travel great distances in air and require very thick . . . materials (such as concrete or water) to block them."[5] Neutrons are the only type of ionizing radiation that can make other matter radioactive. This is because, when the stable atoms of matter are struck by neutron radiation, a proton can be hit and knocked out, since neutrons and protons are about the same size. When that happens, the stable atom is turned into an unstable one that emits ionizing radiation. It is a process that can affect many of the atoms in the matter that is struck. A good way to imagine how this occurs is to think of a billiard game. The balls are atoms, and the cue ball—the penetrating neutron—hits one ball, imparts energy to it, and sends that ball moving; the ball knocks into another ball or two, which strike other balls, and so on, until many "balls" are ionized and emitting radiation. Eventually, all the billiard balls slow and stop, but the radiation is absorbed by the matter that was struck. All four types of ionizing radiation can be destructive to the atoms of matter they penetrate, but neutron particles are the most dangerous to living matter, including human beings, because of their ability to destabilize other atoms and spread radiation.

Ionizing Radiation Types and the Human Body

When a person is exposed to ionizing radiation, the effects and the danger depend on the type of radiation, as well as how the exposure occurred. When ionizing radiation strikes the atoms of the human body and knocks out electrons, the cells that make up the body can be damaged. In the special case of neutron particles, which are very penetrating, subatomic particles in the nucleus may be knocked out, too, and damage the cell. Since alpha particles are so heavy and slow, they cannot penetrate past the outer surface layer of dead skin. When they travel through the air, they are not dangerous to people. Sometimes, however, people may swallow or breathe in alpha particles. Inside the body the radiation can damage nearby cells such as those in the lungs. Beta particles are similar to alpha particles in their dangerousness. They, too, can damage nearby cells when they are swallowed or inhaled, and some of them can penetrate the skin deeply enough to do damage there, also. The skin cells may die and the skin may be reddened or burned. Both alpha and beta particles that get inside the body can cause lung cancer. Because beta particles are smaller and travel further than alpha particles, they also can reach more tissues and organs in the body and increase the risks of other cancers.

Scientists explain that ionizing radiation causes cancer by damaging the deoxyribonucleic acid (DNA) molecules in cells. DNA is the blueprint in each cell that directs its functioning. When the bond that holds a DNA molecule together is disrupted because the atoms that make up the molecule are ionized, the cell may die. If it does not, the blueprint for the cell with its instructions may be damaged and fail to function correctly. Eventually, often over a long period, this DNA error—called a mutation—may cause the cell to divide and grow uncontrollably. This uncontrolled multiplication of cells in the body is called cancer. Cancer, caused by radiation-damaged DNA, is the greatest risk from alpha and beta particles that get inside the body.

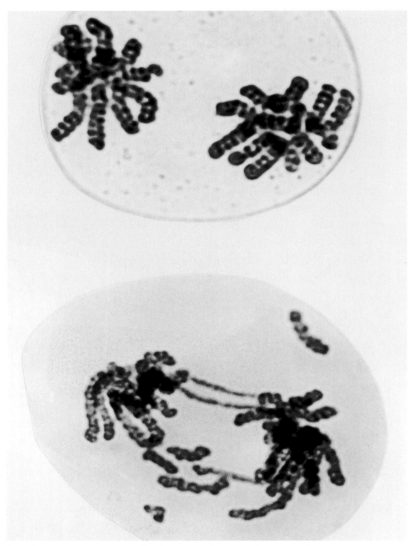

An electron micrograph shows radiation damage done to chromosomes (bottom).

Gamma rays, because they are so penetrating, do not have to be swallowed or inhaled to do damage. As they travel through the air, they easily penetrate the human body and even pass through it. Potentially, says the U.S. Environmental Protection Agency (EPA), uncontrolled exposure to gamma rays could ionize all the organs of the body, severely damaging or killing all the cells and thus killing the exposed individual. The danger posed by gamma radiation exposure is not a risk of cancer in the future because of slow changes to DNA-damaged cells. The damage is immediate. The EPA explains that human exposure to gamma rays can be a serious hazard to life and health. Like gamma rays, neutrons are extremely penetrating, high-energy particles that easily travel into and through the human body. They are also extremely hazardous to living cells and can cause immediate and severe damage to exposed cells.

Measuring Exposure and Dose of Radiation

Even gamma rays and neutron radiation, however, are not always destructive to living things. The damage done by any of the four types of radiation depends on the length of exposure, the amount of radiation received, and which parts of the body received the radiation. In addition, exposure is not the same as the amount of radiation, or dose, received by the body. Exposure may or may not result in the body absorbing a dose of radiation. As the Health Physics Society explains, "If we are exposed and some of the energy from the radiation stays in our body, that is radiation dose. Radiation dose is the energy deposited in our cells and tissues from exposure to radiation."[6] Small doses of radiation are a normal part of the human environment and not harmful. For example, people are exposed to small amounts of gamma rays from cosmic radiation and may be exposed to low levels of alpha and beta particles from the radon gas in the soil. Most often, this radiation does not even strike the atoms of the body, because on the atomic level, people are mostly empty space. Even if one atom of a cell is struck, the effect on the cell can be insignificant. In addition, even a damaged cell often can repair itself. It is a high exposure to a large amount of ionizing radiation that increases the risk of damage to many cells and therefore injury or death to a person.

Scientists have established methods of quantifying both radiation exposure and radiation dose and the health effects

Half-Life

Every radioactive element goes through radioactive decay (where subatomic particles are emitted until the element's atoms are stable), but each element takes a different amount of time to decay and become stable. Scientists describe this rate of decay by measuring half-life. Half-life is the time it takes for half the radioactive atoms to decay. A half-life, depending on the element, might be just a few seconds or could take billions of years. The isotope of americium called americium-241, for example, has a half-life of 458 years. After 458 years, half of its radioactive atoms are stable and no longer emitting radiation. In another 458 years, 25 percent are left (half of the half that was radioactive). After another 458 years, 12.5 percent of its atoms are radioactive, and so on, until after about twenty half-life periods, the element is essentially no longer radioactive.

The half-life of the polonium isotope polonium-215, which is usually human-made, has a half-life of 1.78 milliseconds. (A millisecond is one-thousandth of a second.) Radioactive iodine—which can be released in a nuclear power plant accident—has a half-life of eight days. Uranium has three natural isotopes that have half-lives of 245,000 years, 704 million years, and 4.46 billion years.

These small cubes with one black side representing decayed nuclei are used to simulate the random action of radioactive decay.

on the human body. The International Atomic Energy Agency says, "The effects of radiation at high doses and dose rates are reasonably well documented. A very large dose delivered to the whole body over a short time will result in the death of the exposed person within days. . . . However, at low doses of radiation, there is still considerable uncertainty about the overall effects."[7] Despite the uncertainty, estimates of dosages and effects are based on measurements that are well understood.

Using scientific instruments and monitors, scientists in the United States measure radiation exposure in units called roentgens. A roentgen is a measure of the amount of energy in the air or environment and of gamma rays (although all the types of radiation may be present). Rad (radiation absorbed dose) is a measure of the radiation absorbed by living matter or tissues. A modern measure of absorbed dose is the gray (Gy). One gray equals 100 rad. Rem (roentgen equivalent man) is a measure of the dose of radiation received by a person and considers the amount of the radiation along with the damage it does to living things. Two other measurements used are the millirem (0.001 rem) and the Sievert (Sv), which is equal to 100 rem. As an example of how these measurements are used in everyday life, the EPA states that people receive about 31 millirem of radiation from cosmic sources each year. Radon gas that might seep into the basement of a house would expose a person to about 200 millirem each year. As far as scientists know, these dosage levels are insignificant to a person's health. Even much larger dosages are thought to be safe by experts. For example, on the basis of current knowledge, U.S. law allows for a typical young man working in a nuclear facility such as a power plant to receive 5 rem per year. This amount is not considered to be dangerous, but as rem rises, ionizing radiation can pose a threat to health.

Rem Dosages and Health

As rem increase, the effects on the body depend on whether the dosage is chronic or acute. Chronic means that the radiation dose occurs over a long period. Acute refers to a short-term or onetime radiation dose. The health effects of chronic or acute dosages depend on the rem received and also on whether the whole body or just a part of the body (for instance, a hand or arm) received the ionizing radiation dose. For whole-body exposure, for example, the Health Physics Society explains that 10 rem received either short term or long term would cause no observable health effects. However, such a dose could cause a slight increase in the risk of cancer in the future. With 100 rem received, either over a period of years or all at once, the risk of cancer in the future is significantly increased. In addition, a person who receives an acute dose of 100 rem may suffer cellular damage and health effects, but he or she will be able to recover. When the rem dosage reaches 1,000, the health effects are immediate and severe, and the ionizing radiation dosage is likely to be fatal. In general, any whole-body doses above 50 rem can cause at least some symptoms of illness, while doses above 200 rem cause cell damage and sickness that requires medical help.

Worst-Case Scenarios

When just a part of the body receives the radiation dose, the effects may be very specific. For example, only 40 rem received by the human eye can cause cataracts to form. About 100 rems will cause hair to fall out (on the head or on the body part exposed). The skin on a body part that receives 200 rem is reddened like a sunburn, while skin that receives a dosage above 1,500 rem will blister and burn. Such high rem doses (above 1,000) to a vital organ can lead to severe damage, illness, and death.

The rem dosage levels that are dangerous to humans are almost always due to artificial sources of ionizing radiation. People received these high dosages when the United States dropped atomic bombs on Hiroshima and Nagasaki in Japan during World War II. On other rare occasions, people working in nuclear research and fissioning atoms have accidentally received such doses of ionizing radiation. Rare accidents at nuclear power plants have caused people to receive high

A technician uses a radiation detector to scan and measure a particular material's radioactive properties.

rem doses, as have accidents with radioactive sources used in nuclear medicine. Occasionally, people involved in mining radioactive material such as uranium or processing these materials for use in industry have received high rem dosages, too. In all these situations an acute exposure to a very high dose of ionizing radiation can lead to radiation sickness.

CHAPTER TWO

What Is Radiation Sickness?

Radiation sickness is caused by acute and excessive exposure to ionizing radiation. Popularly, it is called radiation sickness or radiation poisoning, but according to the Centers for Disease Control and Prevention (CDC), the correct medical term is *acute radiation syndrome*, or ARS. The CDC says, "Acute Radiation Syndrome (ARS) . . . is an acute illness caused by irradiation [exposure to ionizing radiation] of the entire body (or most of the body) by a high dose of penetrating radiation in a very short period of time (usually a matter of minutes)."[8] The destructive impact on the cells of the human body causes a variety of symptoms and can lead to death. Doctors and scientists diagnose ARS by its symptoms and determine a prognosis—the eventual outcome and survivability—by measuring dosage levels and exposure time.

Not until the beginning of the nuclear age did scientists come to recognize and understand radiation sickness. Radiation sickness is almost exclusively the result of human-made nuclear radiation. Except for the radiation sickness that occurred after the bombing of Japan in 1945, all other observed cases have happened because of accidents with nuclear material. From experience with these accidents and with atomic bomb victims, scientists have learned what happens to a person who receives an acute dosage of ionizing radiation. They now know that there is a pattern of emerging symptoms that appear in a predictable order. How soon these symptoms appear and how severe they are depends on the dosage level and amount of exposure.

A Case of Radiation Sickness

The first peacetime death from ARS happened on August 21, 1945, in Los Alamos, New Mexico, where scientists had assembled the atomic bombs and continued to research nuclear fission and neutron radiation after World War II ended. The victim's symptoms illustrate the typical course of radiation sickness when high doses of gamma rays and neutron particles strike the human body.

Harry K. Daghlian Jr., a twenty-four-year-old scientist, was performing an experiment with the element plutonium. Plutonium is extremely unstable. With enough of it (called critical mass), scientists can start a chain reaction of neutrons flying off atoms and hitting other atoms until trillions of atoms are exploding and releasing tremendous amounts of energy. Daghlian was performing neutron reflection experiments, in which he surrounded his sphere of plutonium with tungsten carbide bricks. These bricks reflected neutrons split from atoms back into the plutonium sphere in order to intensify the nuclear chain reaction. The closer the bricks came to the plutonium, the more intense was the chain reaction.

While he was adding a brick to his pile with his left hand, Daghlian accidentally dropped the brick onto the plutonium. In those days scientists experimented with radioactive material with their bare hands. They did not perform experiments remotely, with robots or by using tools to manipulate materials from behind protective shields. This modern technology was not available to them. When he dropped the brick, Daghlian knew immediately that he had made a terrible mistake. When the brick touched the plutonium, a full, supercritical chain reaction occurred, with a greatly increasing number of fissioning atoms. Daghlian knocked the brick aside, but it was too late. A Geiger counter in the room, which measures radiation in the air, began to click wildly. There was a bright flash of blue light from the plutonium that filled the room. Daghlian's hand tingled. Later it was determined that he had received a dosage of 5.1 Sv (510 rem) of gamma and neutron radiation to his whole body.

When ARS Occurs

The Centers for Disease Control and Prevention lists five required conditions for an individual to be at risk for ARS. These conditions are:

- The radiation dose must be large (i.e., greater than 0.7 Gray or 70 rads). . . .
- The dose usually must be external (i.e., the source of radiation is outside of the patient's body). . . .
- The radiation must be penetrating (i.e., able to reach the internal organs). High energy X-rays, gamma rays, and neutrons are penetrating radiations.
- The entire body (or a significant portion of it) must have received the dose. . . .
- The dose must have been delivered in a short time (usually a matter of minutes).

Centers for Disease Control and Prevention. "Acute Radiation Syndrome: A Fact Sheet for Physicians." March 18, 2005. www.bt.cdc.gov /radiation/arsphysicianfact sheet.asp.

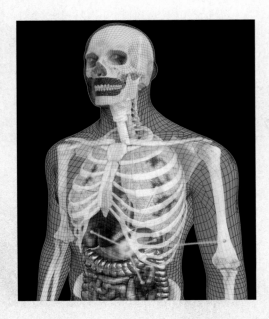

Effects of acute radiation syndrome (ARS) are shown. The stomach is affected first, and other symptoms spread from there.

A fellow scientist took Daghlian to the Los Alamos hospital immediately. Within ninety minutes he began to have symptoms of ARS. His hands swelled and he became nauseated and started vomiting. Scientist Arnold S. Dion, who has researched the accident, says, "The nausea persisted throughout the second day, but without vomiting; instead, he now had to endure prolonged episodes of hiccups. After these initial two days, his appetite returned and he was able to eat well; however, other symptoms soon became apparent."[9] Next Daghlian's skin reddened and blistered, not only on his hands but also on his abdomen. The flesh began to die, and the reddening progressed to his neck and face. By the tenth day he experienced severe stomach pain and cramping whenever he tried to eat. On the twelfth day he developed constant diarrhea. By day fifteen he had a high fever, his blood pressure dropped dangerously low, and his heart raced. Finally, he fell into a coma. Daghlian died on the twenty-sixth day after his radiation accident, with all the skin on his arms, chest, and abdomen burned away, all the hair on his body gone, and a thin, wasted body from lack of food.

Stages of ARS

The progression of Daghlian's illness and death illustrates the four stages of ARS, as described by the CDC. The first is called the prodromal stage. (A prodrome is defined as the early symptom indicating the onset of disease.) During the prodromal stage, the victim's symptoms include nausea, vomiting, anorexia (loss of appetite), and possibly diarrhea. This first stage is followed by the latent stage, during which symptoms seem to disappear and the victim looks and feels healthy. Daghlian, for example, was in this second stage when his appetite returned after two days, and he was able to eat normally. The third stage, the manifest illness stage, is the period of overt illness. The victim suffers organ damage and a severe suppression of the immune system. The immune system is the body's complex system of protecting itself from outside invasion and diseases. During the manifest illness stage, this system breaks down, and infections become likely. The fourth and final stage of ARS is called recovery or death.

Whether a victim dies, how long each stage lasts, and the severity of symptoms directly depends on the dosage of radiation. The higher the dose, the more quickly and severely the

A victim of radiation sickness from the Nagasaki atomic bomb is seen in the manifest illness stage of ARS, where the victim suffers organ damage, skin lesions, and severe suppression of the immune system.

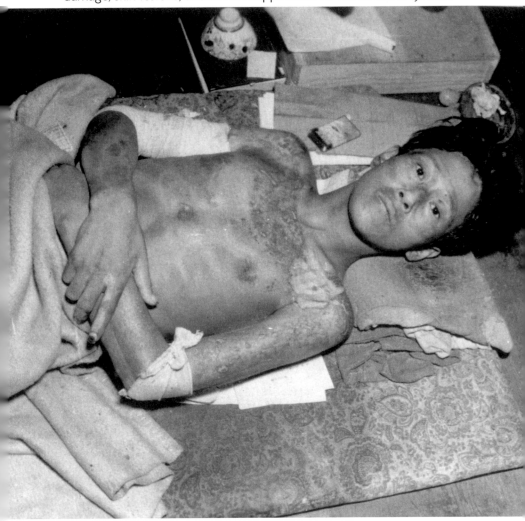

victim experiences each stage. With a high dose such as Daghlian received, for instance, the prodomal stage begins within a few minutes. At a lower dose, the first stage may not appear for several hours. The latent stage may last for just a few hours or may continue for a few weeks. The science information organization Thomson Reuters Integrity explains, "The duration of latency decreases as the radiation dose increases."[10] The manifest illness stage can last for weeks or months. Recovery or death, the final stage, is also dependent on dosage level. Death can occur within hours at extremely high levels, but according to the CDC, those people who do not recover will die within a few months at most. Those who do recover may do so within weeks or take up to two years. At any dosage the order of the symptoms is the same, and the victim goes through each of the four stages, although the length of time for each stage can vary.

The Relationship Between Stages and Dosages

Daghlian took twenty-six days to reach the fourth stage of radiation sickness, but the progression of ARS can be even faster. A second accident with plutonium research at Los Alamos occurred several months later, on May 21, 1946. This accident demonstrates the direct relationship between dosage level and severity and speed of symptoms. In similar circumstances as Daghlian's, Louis P. Slotin was demonstrating plutonium chain reaction techniques to seven people in his laboratory. With a screwdriver, he was holding two spheres of plutonium apart. When the screwdriver slipped, the spheres came together and the plutonium reaction immediately became critical, causing a chain reaction of atomic fission and powerful neutron radiation that flashed throughout the room and caused a wave of heat felt by everyone present. Slotin used his bare hands to separate the spheres and stop the reaction. He then threw his body over the experiment to protect the other people in the room from the neutron radiation. It took less than a second, but Slotin received 2,100 rem, 21 Sv, throughout his whole body. The Oak Ridge Associated Universities, an association for nuclear research, reports that the other seven people in the room received varying rem doses, depending on how close they were to the plutonium. The dosages for them were 360, 250, 160, 110, 65, 47, and 37 rem.

Slotin's symptoms occurred immediately because his dosage level was so high. He experienced a tingling in his hands, a sour taste in his mouth, and then almost immediately vomited as he left the laboratory for the hospital. He knew what was in store for him. When he got to the hospital, he turned to scientist Alvin C. Graves, who had been standing right behind him in the laboratory, and said, "I'm sorry I got you into this. I'm afraid I have less than a 50 per cent chance of living. I hope you have better than that."[11] Within twenty-four hours, Slotin's hands were swollen, burned, and blistered, and he could not use them. His latent stage lasted about two days, similar to the latency that Daghlian experienced. By the fifth day, however, the manifest illness stage left him in severe pain, with organs breaking down, a high fever, and purple skin all over his body. He was in a coma on the eighth day after his accident and died on the ninth day. Because the radiation dosage was so much higher than the fatal dosage Daghlian received, Slotin's symptoms were more severe in a shorter amount of time, and he died more quickly.

Lower Dosages and Surviving the ARS Stages

Nothing could save Slotin from death by radiation sickness, but by his quick actions, he saved everyone else in the room with him. The two men closest to him, however, did suffer radiation sickness. They were Graves, who had received 360 rem, and S. Allan Kline, who received 250 rem. Kline began experiencing nausea and vomiting after a few hours in the hospital. For the next two weeks, he was weak, anorexic, and nauseated. His immune system weakened, his blood pressure dropped, and he had bouts of fever. Then gradually, his body stabilized. When he left the hospital, he was weak and exhausted for months. His hair continued to fall out, and his

Unborn Children and Acute Radiation Exposure

If a pregnant woman is exposed to a high dose of radiation, the unborn baby, or fetus, can be severely damaged even if the mother recovers. Scientists say that fetuses are extremely sensitive to radiation. Scientists believe that during the first twelve weeks of pregnancy, the most likely effect of exposure to a high dosage of radiation is miscarriage and the death of the fetus. Ionizing radiation doses higher than 100 millisieverts (10 rem) that occur between the eighth and fifteenth weeks of pregnancy can cause brain damage to the fetus if it survives. Doses higher than 200 millisieverts (20 rem) that occur between the sixteenth and twenty-fifth weeks cause brain damage, also. At a dose exposure of 1,000 millisieverts (100 rem), the fetus may be born with serious malformations, low birth weight, and mental retardation. At any time during pregnancy, doses above 100 millisieverts (10 rem) may increase the child's future risk of developing cancer.

skin was so sensitive that he could not tolerate any exposure to the sun. He was sterile—unable to father children—for the next two years. He also had to be fired from his job, because it was too dangerous for him to be exposed to any more radiation in his lifetime.

Graves suffered acute radiation sickness and was hospitalized for several weeks. The dosage he received gave him about a fifty-fifty chance of surviving. He experienced the same symptoms as did Kline, including the vomiting, fever, exhaustion, temporary hair loss, and temporary sterility. Graves also suffered a reddening of the skin all over his body and permanent damage to his eyes. Nevertheless, his fourth stage was recovery, not death.

Alvin C. Graves, pictured at an atomic bomb test site in 1955, survived his bout of acute radiation syndrome that resulted from a nuclear accident in 1946.

What Causes the Symptoms of Radiation Sickness?

All of the symptoms of radiation sickness, whether the victim dies or recovers, can be explained by the cell damage that is the inevitable result of ionizing radiation. The severity of sickness depends on the amount of cell damage that occurs and where in the body it occurs. The areas of the body that are the most vulnerable to radiation are bone marrow in the centers of bones, where blood cells are manufactured; cells lining the gastrointestinal tract (the stomach and intestines); cells of the eyes, hair, and skin; and cells of the nerves and blood vessels. The cells in these body structures are known to be rapidly dividing cells, which means that the body is frequently replacing these cells with new ones through the process of cell division. When these cells are struck by high-energy radiation, they will be so damaged that they are destroyed by the heat of the radiation.

The higher the radiation dose, the more cells are killed. If enough cells are killed and cannot be replaced by the body fast enough, the body organs themselves will die. If the radiation dose is damaging but not lethal, eventually the body can make new cells to repair itself. This is what happened, for example, with the hair cells of Graves and Kline. They both lost their hair temporarily, but as their bodies recovered and began making new hair cells, the hair grew back. When the cells killed are in essential organs, such as the stomach or bone marrow, such recovery may or may not be possible.

ARS and Organ Damage

The CDC says that there are three major ARS syndromes, in which all four stages of radiation sickness occur with symptoms and body damage specific to the syndrome that develops. The first is bone marrow syndrome. It is characterized by the destruction of the bone marrow cells that manufacture blood cells, such as red blood cells, white blood cells, and platelets. The CDC explains, "The survival rate of patients with this syndrome decreases with increasing dose. The primary cause of death is the destruction of the bone marrow, resulting in infection and hemorrhage."[12] Infection is the result of the loss of white blood cells, or lymphocytes, which are a major component of the immune system. Hemorrhage is excessive bleeding from the blood vessels and is caused by the loss of the platelets that form clots and control bleeding. Red blood cell loss causes anemia (low iron levels in the blood), weakness, and fainting. People can survive this syndrome. Graves, for example, gradually recovered from his radiation sickness as his bone marrow slowly began to generate new white blood cells, red blood cells, and platelets. In the modern measurement using grays, this syndrome occurs when the dosage level is between 0.7 and 10 Gy (70 to 1,000 rads).

Gastrointestinal syndrome occurs with a dose of about 10 Gy (1,000 rads). This is the syndrome that led to the abdominal pain, prolonged vomiting, diarrhea, and anorexia that Slotin and Daghlian experienced because so many cells in their stomachs and intestines were killed. It is also what caused their deaths. The CDC says, "Survival is extremely unlikely with this syndrome. Destructive and irreparable changes in the GI [gastrointestinal] tract and bone marrow usually cause infection, dehydration, and electrolyte imbalance. Death usually

Types and Severity of Symptoms of Acute Radiation Syndrome

Symptoms and Treatment Strategy		Mild (1–2 gray [Gy])	Moderate (2–4Gy)	Severe (4–6Gy)	Very Severe (6–8Gy)	Lethal (>8Gy)
Vomiting	Onset Incidence	After 2 hours (hrs) 10–50%	After 1–2 hrs 70–90%	Within 1 hr 100%	Within 30 min 100%	Within 10 min 100%
Diarrhea	Onset Incidence	None	None	Mild 3–8 hrs <10%	Heavy 1–8 hrs >10%	Heavy within minutes–1 hr almost 100%
Headache	Onset Incidence	Slight	Mild	Moderate 4–24 hrs 50%	Severe 3–4 hrs 80%	Severe 1–2 hrs 80-90%
Change in Consciousness Levels	Onset Incidence	Alert	Alert	Alert	Possibility of impairment	Unconsciousness by order of seconds or minutes Seconds–minutes 100% (>50Gy)
Change in Body Temperature	Onset Incidence	Normal	Increased 1–3 hrs 10–80%	Fever 1–2 hrs 80–100%	High fever <1hrs 100%	High fever <1 hrs 100%
Treatment Strategy		Outpatient observation	Observation at general hospital; treatment at specialized hospital, if required	Treatment at specialized hospital	Treatment at specialized hospital	Palliative treatment (advanced medical care, including stem cell transplantation)

Taken from: IAEA/WHO Safety Report Series. www.remnet.jp/englisa/lecture/b03_04/e_003.html.

occurs within 2 weeks."[13] Dehydration is the loss of water and essential salts and minerals (electrolytes) that are critical for body functioning. Some people can live longer or even recover from this syndrome, especially if the dosage level that causes the symptoms is lower than 10 Gy or if they receive medical help. Gastrointestinal cells can slowly be replaced by the body, but often the victim dies of complications before this happens.

The most destructive ARS syndrome is called cardiovascular/central nervous system syndrome. This syndrome is caused by a radiation dose above 50 Gy (5,000 rads). With this dosage the entire circulatory system—including the blood vessels and heart—collapses. Every organ of the body is devastated, and severe symptoms, including unconsciousness, appear within minutes. No latent stage occurs, and the syndrome is always fatal. Death may occur within hours but always occurs within three days.

The system for classifying ARS syndromes was developed during the late 1950s, and medical doctors around the world today use it to diagnose radiation sickness and to determine the prognosis for anyone exposed to a high dose of radiation. Since skin damage from radiation usually goes along with all three syndromes, medical professionals also consider cutaneous radiation syndrome to be a part of ARS. It refers to all the skin symptoms that may affect a victim, including reddening, blistering, burns, hair loss, ulcers, and wounds to the skin. Usually, this syndrome heals on its own as skin cells are replaced, but doctors may observe skin changes to help them make a diagnosis of ARS.

Diagnosing ARS by Determining Radiation Dosage

Diagnosing radiation sickness is relatively straightforward when the level of exposure is known. In most circumstances in which an individual is at risk for exposure (such as in a lab or a nuclear power plant), instruments are regularly used to monitor radiation. In addition to Geiger counters, dosimeter badges—worn by every person working around radiation—record the radiation accumulated by the person on an ongoing basis. These instruments give a doctor an accurate reading of dosage in rem, Sv, or Gy if an accident occurs. In addition, the doctor can interview the victim or others in the area in order to determine what radiation was released in the environment. With a known radiation dose, doctors know with some certainty what symptoms and disease progression to expect.

When the dosage level is uncertain, the doctor may observe the victim for prodromal symptoms. The time until the onset of vomiting is a good rough measure of dosage received. The sooner the victim vomits, the higher the dose. Thomson Reuters Integrity explains, for example, that vomiting occurs in

In addition to Geiger counters, dosimeter badges record the radiation accumulated by a person working around radioactive materials.

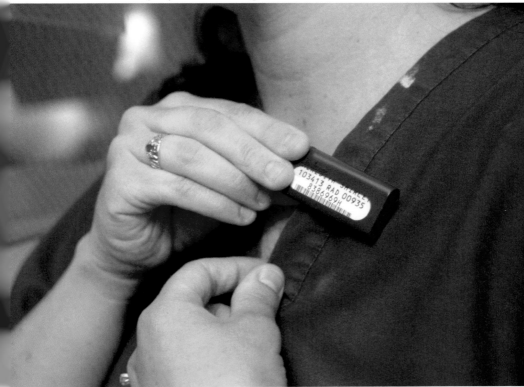

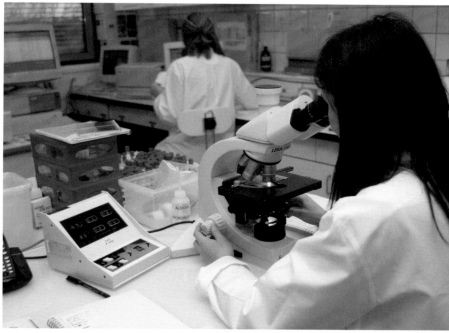

A laboratory technician does a white blood cell test to estimate the radiation level of a person in the initial hours after radiation exposure.

less than ten minutes at a dosage level of 8 Gy or higher, while vomiting after two hours (or never) indicates a dosage level of less than 2 Gy.

The best quick estimate of radiation dose is a blood test called the complete blood count. In the hours after radiation exposure, the doctor draws blood every two to three hours and counts the lymphocytes in the sample. These white blood cells are short-lived and must be continually replaced in the bone marrow. In the hours after radiation exposure, the white blood cell count drops precipitously for high radiation dosages. Measuring the speed and amount of this drop gives the doctor an estimate of overall radiation received. In addition, the blood is tested every four to six hours over the next two or three days. The lower the lymphocyte count over this period, the higher the radiation dose.

Prognosis and Radiation Dosage

The estimate of radiation dose also provides medical doctors with a prognosis. *The Merck Manual*, a guide for health-care providers, explains how the relationship works. In adults a lymphocyte count that is 1,500 or greater (the number of lymphocyte cells per milliliter of blood) suggests an absorbed radiation dose less than 0.4 Gy. The prognosis is excellent because the body can recover. A lymphocyte count of 1,000 to 1,499 indicates a radiation dosage between 0.5 and 1.9 Gy, and the prognosis is good. With a count between 500 and 999, the dose is estimated to be between 2 to 3.9 Gy, and the prognosis is fair. This means significant ARS, but the victim may recover. At a lymphocyte count of 100 to 499, the estimated dosage is 4 to 7.9 Gy, and the prognosis is poor. Severe ARS is expected, and many victims will not survive. Lymphocyte counts below 100 indicate dosages greater than 8 Gy and are almost always fatal.

The prognosis for radiation sickness is a critical part of the diagnosis because it tells doctors what symptoms to expect and how likely it is that the victim will survive. Researchers have determined that with medical care, about 50 percent of victims receiving 6 Gy dosages can recover, while a few people with even 10 Gy dosages can survive. Without medical care, about half of people receiving 3 Gy will die, and a dosage level of 6 Gy is almost always fatal. Although medical treatment cannot save all people with ARS, it is essential for most victims of radiation sickness and gives them the best chance of recovery.

CHAPTER THREE

Treatment of Radiation Sickness

When the medical world faced the first victims of radiation sickness, doctors knew very little about how to help them. When the Hiroshima and Nagasaki bombs were dropped, no one even suspected that those who survived the blasts would fall victim to radiation sickness, much less knew how to treat them. Today, based on scientific studies of atomic bombing victims and the few victims of the rare nuclear accidents that have occurred since 1945, doctors understand what radiation sickness is and have gained knowledge about how to respond medically to the devastating syndrome. Hospitalized victims of acute radiation syndrome (ARS) may still die because there is no known cure, but medical treatment is available for some symptoms of ARS, and with medical support, some people can survive and successfully recover. In general, the Mayo Clinic explains, "Radiation sickness treatment is aimed at preventing further radioactive contamination, managing organ damage, reducing symptoms and managing pain."[14]

Decontamination

The first priority in managing radiation sickness is decontaminating (removing any contaminating radioactive material from) the victim, both externally and internally (outside and inside the body). External decontamination is necessary because neutron radiation can make other matter radioactive and because some radioactive particles can stick to matter. External decontamination means removing any radioactive particles that have been deposited on the body, such as on the skin, hair, and clothing. Decontaminating the victim protects him or her from absorbing an increasing radiation dose and also protects people

External decontamination removes any radioactive particles that have been deposited on the body and helps prevent further absorption of radiation.

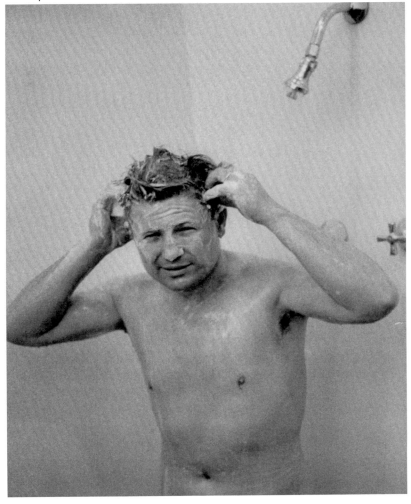

treating and coming in contact with the victim from absorbing radiation themselves. The first step of external decontamination is getting rid of the victim's clothing. The Mayo Clinic staff explains, "Removing clothing and shoes eliminates about 90 percent of external contamination."[15] Then doctors may examine the whole body with an instrument known as a Geiger-Müller probe. This probe is an extra-sensitive instrument for detecting radiation. It has a long handle so that the person using the detector can be a bit distant from the victim, and it can detect alpha, beta, and gamma radiation.

If radioactivity is present or suspected to be present on the victim's body, doctors gently wash the victim with soap and warm water. Alternatively, if the victim is able, he or she can take a shower and scrub down with soap or a mild detergent. Any open wounds on the victim's body are cleaned with a sponge and a saline solution (sodium chloride and distilled water). *The Merck Manual* says, "Special attention is usually required for fingernails and skinfolds. Hair that remains contaminated is removed with scissors or electric clippers; shaving is avoided [because skin could be injured]. Inducing sweating (e.g., placing a rubber glove over a contaminated hand) may help remove residual skin contamination."[16] Cleaning and washing may be repeated as necessary to ensure that the radioactive particles have been removed.

While performing initial decontamination, medical professionals have to protect themselves and the hospital. Treatment takes place in an isolation area of the hospital, where no one enters except people involved in the treatment of the victim. Medical personnel in the isolated area wear gowns, gloves, masks, shoe coverings, and caps on their heads. They may cover all the equipment in the room with plastic (later to be discarded) and discard the victim's clothing and anything else that contacted the victim—such as sponges, hair clippings, or soap—in special containers that are marked "Caution: Radioactive Material." In addition, *The Merck Manual* recommends that ideally, all medical personnel should wear dosimeter badges to measure any radiation exposure.

External Decontamination
of an Accident Victim

Radiation accident victim Harold McCluskey is an example of a person who underwent external decontamination procedures as the first step in saving his life. In 1976 McCluskey was sixty-four years old and a chemical engineer at the Hanford Plutonium Finishing Plant in Washington State. Behind a Plexiglas shield, he was working with a container in the research facility that held the radioactive, human-made element americium. Americium emits primarily alpha particles but also some gamma rays. The americium in the container was mixed with resin beads and nitric acid (which is poisonous). The container exploded and shattered the shield, and McCluskey was hit with the chemical mixture on the right side of his head, face, neck, and shoulder. Pieces of Plexiglas and metal from the container also drove into his skin. He fell and called out, "I can't see."[17] A coworker pulled him out of the room, and other workers in the plant immediately started wiping his body with damp cloths in order to remove as many radioactive alpha particles as they could as quickly as possible.

A plastic-lined ambulance carried McCluskey to the special Emergency Decontamination and Treatment Facility maintained by the Hanford plant. He was placed in an isolation room that was shielded with concrete and steel and draped in plastic. The medical personnel treating him wore full protective gear. This included respirators for breathing because the alpha particles from McCluskey's body contaminated the air around him. The doctors began external decontamination procedures immediately with a shower. McCluskey's skin was burned by the acid, so washing his body was painful. The doctor in charge of his treatment, Bryce Breitenstein, allowed McCluskey to wash himself with a soft cloth and soap while the medical professionals watched. The scrubbing had to be done repeatedly over the next several weeks because it was impossible to get rid of all the radioactive particles in one session. As well as he could, Breitenstein carefully picked out the metal, plastic, and americium embedded in McCluskey's skin. He

Iodine for Possible Radiation Exposure

In 2011 an accident at a nuclear power plant in Fukushima, Japan, caused a release of radioactivity to the surrounding environment. While workers inside the plant acted to control the radiation release, the Japanese government immediately ordered an evacuation of everyone living within 12.4 miles (20km) of the power plant. As an additional safety measure, the government issued more than two hundred thousand iodine tablets and liquid doses to the evacuation centers. The iodine would protect people's thyroid gland if they were exposed to radioactive iodine. Daily doses can prevent thyroid glands from absorbing the radioactive iodine in the environment. No one was sure that the iodine treatment was necessary, but Japanese medical experts believed the treatment might be helpful, and they did not want to wait to find out if the evacuees were at risk. Even if the iodine pills were unneeded, they would do no harm, since iodine is a normal part of the human diet. Generally, iodine is used to prevent a harmful dose of radiation from being absorbed, rather than to treat people already showing signs of radiation exposure.

A Japanese civic official passes out iodine tablets to the local population.

flushed McCluskey's eyes with saline solution. McCluskey had inhaled, swallowed, and been pierced through the skin with so much direct alpha radiation that Breitenstein feared his patient would die and gave him only a fifty-fifty chance of survival.

Internal Decontamination Procedures

Despite his misgivings, Breitenstein was determined to treat McCluskey aggressively and give him the best chance of survival. The doctor began internal decontamination treatment immediately. Internal decontamination is the effort to remove from the body any radioactive particles that have been absorbed, ingested, or inhaled. Treatment may include inducing vomiting, flushing the eyes and mouth with saline solutions, using medicines to help the body excrete the radioactive particles, or using medicines that prevent the body tissues from absorbing the radiation. The treatment chosen depends on the type of radioactive material to which the victim was exposed. Some radiation accidents—for example, at a nuclear power plant—may involve the release of radioactive iodine. Iodine is easily absorbed by the human thyroid gland. In order to protect the thyroid gland of a victim with this kind of exposure, doctors treat the victim with potassium iodide, a nonradioactive, stable iodine. It fills up the thyroid gland so that the radioactive iodine has nowhere to go and is excreted in the urine. With metals such as americium, plutonium, and arsenic, a chemical compound called a chelating agent is used to help the body excrete the metal. A chelating agent grabs onto the ions of the metal (including the radioactive ions of americium) and binds with them. This process traps the toxic metal so that it can then be excreted in the person's urine.

Breitenstein treated McCluskey with chelation therapy to reduce the radioactivity in his body. The chelating agent was administered through a needle inserted into a vein (an IV). The treatment was repeated numerous times, and after about sixty days, most of the americium was excreted from his body. He survived and was no longer radioactive or a danger to others, and he was able to leave the hospital and live a normal life.

Nevertheless, McCluskey continued to receive this treatment occasionally for about the next five years, and it reduced the radioactivity in his body an estimated one thousand times.

Chelation therapy saved McCluskey's life, but it is a successful treatment method only when radiation contamination is a result of metal particles such as americium. It is of no use with gamma ray or neutron radiation. Fortunately for McCluskey,

This pump injects a chemical into a patient as part of chelation therapy, which helps extract high metal content from the body.

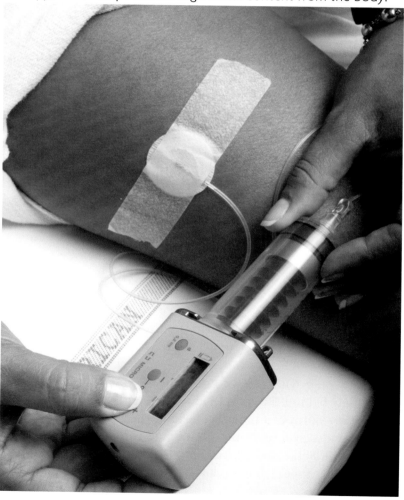

his radiation accident did not involve neutron radiation, and the gamma rays he received were not enough to cause full-blown radiation sickness. Although he absorbed an estimated 18 Gy dosage to his bones and about 8 Gy in his liver, most of the radiation was removed with chelation therapy before it could cause organ damage. Initially, McCluskey did suffer a drop in his lymphocytes, but his body recovered on its own.

Managing Radiation Sickness and Bone Marrow Syndrome

When managing and treating organ damage in a victim of ARS with bone marrow syndrome or gastrointestinal syndrome, doctors do not have the option of employing internal decontamination. These syndromes are usually caused by neutron particles or gamma radiation. The particles or waves have penetrated and passed through the body, and the internal damage is done. If the victim has been exposed to contaminating metallic radiation as well as penetrating neutron or gamma radiation, then internal decontamination is done, but it cannot treat the ARS syndromes. Instead, doctors treat the victim with medicines and procedures meant to support the organs and protect them until the victim's body can begin to recover from the gamma and/or neutron assault. When blood tests indicate a serious drop in lymphocytes, for instance, doctors administer a medicine that increases white blood cell production in the bone marrow. It is a protein called granulocyte colony-stimulating factor.

This medicine was first used to treat ARS in 1987 with victims of an accidental radiation exposure in Goiânia, Brazil. In this incident a clinic that performed radiation therapy to kill cancer cells in people with cancer was shut down. The personnel in charge left behind the therapy machine with its capsule of the radioactive isotope of the metallic element caesium chloride inside. Two men went into the abandoned clinic to look for scrap metal to sell and took the machine. At home they broke it into pieces, broke open the capsule, and exposed the radioactive caesium chloride. Then they sold their find at a junkyard. The

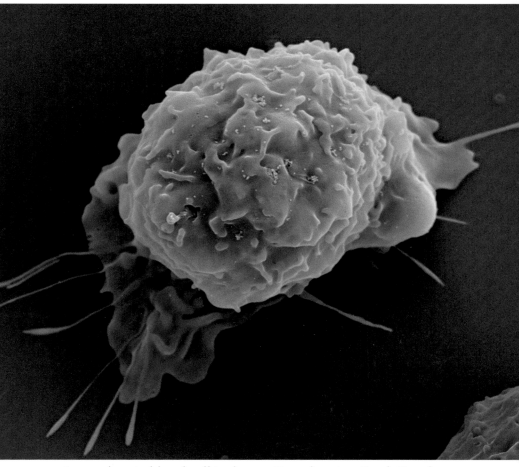

A granulocyte blood cell is shown. Granulocyte-stimulating drugs are used to increase white blood cell production.

junkyard's owner saw the blue glow of the radiation from the exposed capsule, but he did not know that it was dangerous. He admired it and showed it to other people in the neighborhood. Next, says an International Atomic Energy Agency (IAEA) report of the time, a friend "with the aid of a screwdriver removed some fragments of the [radioactive] source from the capsule. These were about the size of rice grains, but readily crumbled into powder." The pretty powder was given as gifts to many friends and family members. The IAEA says, "Subsequently there were several instances of people daubing the radioactive powder on their skin, as with the glitter used at carnival time."[18] In the end 249 people received some level of radiation exposure through contact with the caesium chloride.

Of the people exposed to the radioactivity, at least eleven developed ARS. They had received beta radiation that caused skin damage and gamma radiation that caused internal damage, with absorbed dosages between 1 Gy and 7 Gy. After initial decontamination treatment, the medical team caring for these people administered granulocyte colony-stimulating factor to eight of these people in the hope that it would save their lives. Four of the victims died anyway, because of infections and hemorrhaging, but the other four survived. At that time, the doctors were not sure if the medicine had been beneficial, but today doctors know that the medicine does increase white blood cell production in the bone marrow and therefore may help prevent deadly infections by strengthening the immune system. Granulocyte colony-stimulating factor is always recommended today for victims of bone marrow syndrome.

Severe Bone Marrow Syndrome Treatments

Other medical treatments for bone marrow syndrome, depending on how serious it is, include red blood cell transfusions and platelet transfusions. Transfusions are processes for transferring whole blood or blood components from donors to other persons. These transfusions help prevent anemia and increase the blood's clotting ability, which helps prevent hemorrhaging.

If a victim has severe bone marrow syndrome and doctors determine that the damage to the bone marrow is complete and irreversible, the doctors may consider performing a bone marrow transplant to save the person's life. In a bone marrow transplant, bone marrow is extracted from a donor and then transplanted into the patient. This procedure can be done only if the donor genetically matches the person receiving the marrow and has the same kind of tissue type. Otherwise, the donated bone marrow will be rejected by the body of the recipient. The donor white blood cells can even kill a radiation victim because these added immune system cells might identify the victim's cells as foreign invaders that must be attacked and killed. If a bone marrow transplant is successful, however, the victim may begin to manufacture new blood cells. This procedure works because the immature cells in the marrow—called stem cells—generate new blood cells and repopulate the victim's body with healthy cells. Despite the potential benefits of a bone marrow transplant, the procedure is risky and the outcome uncertain. Radiation expert A.E. Baranov of the IAEA recommends that "bone marrow transplants should be carried out only in patients who have received whole body doses of gamma radiation of 9.0 Gy or

Bone marrow is harvested from a donor for a transplant. Radiation sickness victims may need such transplants to survive.

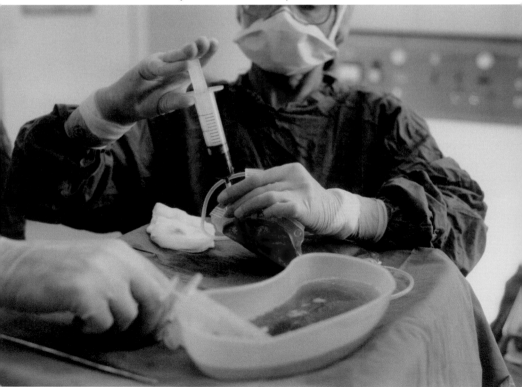

When Radiation Was "Good" for You

After radiation was discovered in the early 1900s, many people and doctors alike theorized that radiation was natural, healthy, and good for one's aches and pains. Quack medicines (untested and usually fraudulent) were developed and sold that contained radio-active elements. One such medicine was Radithor, a liquid medicine that contained a high amount of radium. A wealthy businessperson named Eben McBurney Byers took the medicine on the advice of his doctor in 1927, when pain in his arm from a fall would not go away. He did not use just one bottle, however. He drank three bottles a day for three years. By 1930, when Byers gave up the medicine, he had so much radium accumulated in his body that his bones were disintegrating and holes were eaten in his brain. He died of radium poisoning in 1932. To announce his death, the *Wall Street Journal* ran the headline: "The Radium Water Worked Fine Until His Jaw Came Off." In large part because of Byers's suffering and death, the new U.S. Food and Drug Administration (FDA) demanded that makers of radioactive medicines prove their safety and effectiveness or be prosecuted. That ruling ended the era of using radiation as a cure for anything.

Quoted in Theodore Gray. "For That Healthy Glow, Drink Radiation!" *PopSci*, August 17, 2004. www.popsci.com/scitech/article/2004-08/healthy-glow-drink-radiation.

Radithor "certified radioactive water" was meant to heal but instead caused patients to die from radiation poisoning.

more."[19] At a dosage of this level, the victim is almost certain to die despite other medical treatment, and so the transplant is worth the risk.

Treatment for Gastrointestinal Syndrome

For gastrointestinal syndrome, in which the cells in the stomach and intestines die, medical treatment cannot restore or replace the dead and dying cells. Instead, doctors try to support the victim by trying to prevent further damage. They give the victim fluids by IV along with electrolytes (electrically charged minerals found in many body fluids) to prevent dehydration and attempt to restore the electrolyte balance in the body. They also treat the victim with intravenous nutrition, which is called total parenteral nutrition. (Parenteral means outside the gastrointestinal system.) This treatment involves giving nutrition as a liquid food mixture through an IV. It allows the stomach and intestines to rest completely but still provides the body with the proteins, carbohydrates, fats, vitamins, and minerals that it needs to function and repair itself.

Despite medical treatment, however, most people with gastrointestinal syndrome die within two weeks of exposure. Treatment cannot stop or reverse the death of cells in the stomach and intestines, and these organs may be irreparably damaged. First to die are the cells in the mucous lining of the gastrointestinal tract. This damage is what causes nausea, vomiting, and diarrhea. Even if doctors can stop the vomiting and diarrhea, cells in the intestine usually begin to die. This cell death leads to infection because the bacteria that normally live in the intestines can no longer be prevented from multiplying and escaping to other body organs. A typical complication of bacterial infection is sepsis, which is a whole-body inflammation that occurs when the immune system tries to fight an overwhelming infection. The inflammation blocks oxygen and nutrients from reaching body organs, and they die. Very often, doctors cannot prevent or successfully fight sepsis, and the organ death leads to death for the victim.

General ARS Symptom Treatments

In all cases of ARS, medical treatment involves treating the symptoms of vomiting, diarrhea, and shock, as well as dealing with or preventing infections. Vomiting and diarrhea are treated with antiemetic and antidiarrheal drugs. Broad spectrum antibiotics (which are effective against a wide range of bacteria) are used to prevent and treat infections. If necessary, antiviral and antifungal drugs are a part of protecting the victim from infection, too. Medicines to reduce fevers are commonly prescribed. Shock is a whole-body response to trauma in which the cells do not get enough oxygen or nutrients. Shock can occur when there are not enough red blood cells to carry oxygen to body cells, when dehydration reduces the plasma (or blood fluid) in the blood vessels, or when blood vessels themselves become weak and leak fluid from sepsis, which means nutrients carried in the bloodstream cannot reach body cells. If allowed to continue, shock can quickly lead to organ failure and death. If a victim of ARS is at risk of shock, doctors treat with oxygen, medicines to raise blood pressure (to get more blood to body tissues), and blood transfusions if hemorrhage is suspected.

Shock and infection are also a danger with the cutaneous radiation syndrome that accompanies ARS, because severe skin burns are possible. Skin is the primary body defense against foreign invaders such as bacteria and viruses. Skin that is severely burned is destroyed and cannot prevent invaders from entering the body. Infections are the likely outcome. In addition, severe burns can affect the skin's blood vessels and cause them to leak plasma. If enough fluid is lost, shock can be the result. Skin wounds are gently washed with cool water, and the burns may be treated with burn creams and medicines applied to the inflamed skin. As with other radiation sickness treatments, antibiotics to prevent infection and medications to control pain are important parts of medical care. If the victim recovers from ARS, further treatment for the burns, such as skin grafts to replace destroyed skin and therapy exercises to restore normal motion to body parts such as arms and legs, may be necessary. At times, amputation of limbs, toes, or fingers may be required if the burns have caused death of the tissues in these areas.

Treating Pain and Suffering

Whatever symptoms arise, doctors try to respond with treatment that manages symptoms and helps the victim make it through the syndrome without permanent damage and without undue suffering. Medicines that reduce or stop nausea and vomiting, for example, are valuable not only to prevent these symptoms from harming the body but also to reduce suffering. Medicines that treat pain are critical for relieving suffering, too. When the absorbed radiation dose is so high that no treatment can help the victim to survive, doctors concentrate on easing suffering. This is called end-of-life care. Its goal is to make the victim as comfortable as possible. The Mayo Clinic explains, "Depending on the severity of illness, death can occur within two days or two weeks. People with a lethal radiation dose will receive medications to control pain, nausea, vomiting and diarrhea. They may also benefit from psychological or pastoral care."[20] Pain control may include use of morphine given through an IV and sedatives to help the victim relax and sleep. If the victim is conscious and alert, a psychiatrist or psychologist may talk with him or her in order to help the victim deal with the grief and fear that are likely when a person is facing death. Sometimes, a religious or spiritual counselor may participate in the care, too, in order to comfort and counsel the victim.

In the past doctors have worked aggressively to keep ARS victims alive, even when there was no hope of recovery. In 1999 in Tokaimura, Japan, for example, an accident at a nuclear power facility exposed three men to high amounts of gamma and neutron radiation. One of these men, thirty-five-year-old Hiroshi Ouchi, received a lethal dose of radiation. At the University of Tokyo Hospital, a team of doctors tried every treatment possible to prolong his life, even though they knew that he had received a fatal radiation dose. Ouchi was given a bone marrow transplant with stem cells to grow new blood

People sustaining a lethal radiation dose receive medications
to control pain, nausea, vomiting, and diarrhea. Morphine and
sedatives are used to alleviate pain and help the victim sleep.

cells, massive doses of antibiotics, fluid replacements, skin
grafts, blood transfusions, and medicines to support his body
organs. As his organs began to fail, doctors tried to keep him
alive artificially with machines that kept his heart beating after
he had heart attacks and breathed for him after his own lungs
shut down. Because of all the medical interventions, Ouchi did
not die until eighty-three days after the accident.

    Today the aggressive treatment approach that Ouchi re-
ceived is no longer considered appropriate. ARS experts Jamie
K. Waselenko and his medical team write, "People with a high
exposure dose whose outcome is grim must be identified for
appropriate management. Since there is no chance for survival
after irradiation with a dose of more than 10 to 12 Gy, it is

appropriate for definitive care to be withheld from such individuals. Rather than being treated aggressively, these patients should be provided with comfort measures."[21] In other words, when survival is not possible, doctors do not treat symptoms such as a loss of lymphocytes to try to help the victim recover. Instead, they concentrate on relieving symptoms that cause discomfort and pain and allow the victim to die without invasive medical intervention. Waselenko's team also recommends that the victim's family and loved ones receive psychological support, comfort, and care in such a traumatic situation.

A Terrible Sickness for Everyone

Acute radiation syndrome is traumatic whether the victim recovers or dies. It means a significant amount of physical pain, as well as the emotional pain of dealing with a sickness with an uncertain outcome. Family and loved ones suffer psychologically, too, as they wait to find out if the victim will survive. Radiation sickness is a frightening, often horrific illness that can be extremely difficult for anyone to endure.

CHAPTER FOUR

Life After Radiation Sickness

Even when people get the best medical treatment, radiation sickness can mean a lot of suffering. Many victims of acute radiation syndrome, or ARS, cope with their symptoms with courage and do their best to fight for life and endure their ordeal with dignity. For some, death is inevitable. For others, there is hope and recovery, but recovery may not end their troubles. People who experience radiation sickness can suffer emotionally and psychologically as well as physically and may face a number of unique challenges even after the radiation event is over. The aftermath of radiation exposure can mean an uncertain future for those who become ill or for a city as it attempts to rebuild after an event. People may fear future illnesses as a result of radiation exposure. Sometimes radiation survivors may face rejection by the society they live in or by their families. Other times survivors may be regarded as heroes for their bravery in knowingly exposing themselves to radiation and risking their lives in their pursuit of helping others to safety or preventing a larger disaster. In the case of some radiation events, survivors have been heroic in their willingness to speak out about their ordeal or to submit to medical research procedures to help scientists better understand radiation sickness and its aftermath.

The Chernobyl Disaster

The ordeals of the people of Ukraine who endured the world's worst-ever accidental nuclear disaster are representative of both the suffering and heroism of radiation victims. On April 26, 1986, a nuclear reactor at the Chernobyl nuclear power plant in what is now Ukraine but was then a part of the Union of Soviet Socialist Republics (USSR) was destroyed by a series of explosions. The explosions were caused by an electrical experiment conducted at the plant by scientists who were not experts in nuclear power and did not follow safety rules. The experimenters allowed the water used to cool down the nuclear reactors to overheat and turn to steam. Then the nuclear reactors overheated, and hot nuclear fuel flew into the air with the steam explosions. Massive amounts of radioactive material, including radioactive isotopes of caesium, iodine, strontium, americium, and plutonium, were released.

Most of the radioactive particles fell around the plant itself and on the surrounding countryside. The underlying cause of the accident, according to U.S. nuclear scientists, was that the power plant was poorly designed, had inadequate safeguards, and was staffed, in part, by people lacking the training to prevent such mishaps. The explosions caused major fires, smoke plumes, hot air, and a cloud of fumes that spewed out radioactive materials from the nuclear core that generated the plant's power. The radioactivity was highest at the plant itself and progressively lessened as the distance from the power plant increased. Ukraine, Belarus (the neighboring country along the border, where most of the contamination occurred), and Russia are still coping with and assessing the long-term effects of the radiation exposure on people and the earth today. The short-term effects that occurred immediately after the accident, however, were obvious. In the first days of the disaster, at least 134 people developed ARS, and 28 of these people died. For the most part, the Chernobyl ARS victims were the emergency workers who first responded to the accident. In many cases these people did not understand the danger of radiation and were unwitting victims who did not choose their fate. Their suffering was horrific.

On April 26, 1986, a nuclear reactor at the Chernobyl nuclear plant in Ukraine exploded, throwing massive amounts of radioactive material into the air. The long-term effects of the disaster are still not completely known.

A Firefighter's Suffering and Death

Vasily Ignatenko, for example, was a firefighter in the village of Pripyat, very near the Chernobyl power plant. He lived in a dormitory above the firehouse with his new wife, Lyudmilla. On the night that the Chernobyl accident occurred, Vasily and the other firefighters were some of the first to race toward the fire and try to put it out. They did not succeed. (The fire burned uncontrollably for the next ten days.) Lyudmilla remembers, "Everything was radiant. The whole sky. A tall flame. And smoke. The heat was awful." The firefighters climbed onto the roof of the nuclear reactor to put out the fire. Lyudmilla continues, "He [Vasily] said later it was like walking on tar. They tried to beat down the flames. . . . They weren't wearing canvas gear. They went off just as they were, in their shirt sleeves. No one told them. They had been called for a fire, that was it."[22]

Vasily absorbed a massive, lethal radiation dose and by morning was in the local hospital, vomiting, with fainting spells and a swollen, bloated body. He and the other exposed victims were transferred to a special hospital in Moscow, Russia, where they were isolated, treated, and cared for, but no medical treatment could save them. They were not decontaminated. The political situation in the USSR (which initially denied the extent of the radiation emergency) prevented hospitals and doctors from having appropriate medical facilities or openly carrying out the best treatment and decontamination techniques. Still, hospital staff knew that the victims were highly radioactive. They coped by evacuating the floors above and below the victims to avoid contaminating other patients. Lyudmilla, however, was allowed to stay by her husband's side and spent the next fourteen days watching him die of radiation sickness. It was a horrible ordeal of increasingly devastating symptoms, and it was terrible to watch. Lyudmilla says, "He started to change—every day I met a brand new person."[23] Vasily's skin began to show radiation burns, and sores appeared in his mouth. His skin started to break down. He had diarrhea twenty to thirty times a day. Doctors tried a bone marrow transplant with bone marrow from his sister, but it did not work, and his blood cell counts continued to drop. His hair fell out in clumps, and boils appeared all over his body.

By the end, Lyudmilla remembers, Vasily lay naked and fragile with only one thin sheet covering him. She says, "I changed that little sheet every day, and every day by evening it was covered in blood. I pick him up, and there are pieces of his skin on my hand, they stick to my hands. . . . Any little wrinkle [in his bedding], that was already a wound on him. I clipped my nails down till they bled so I wouldn't accidentally cut him."[24] When Vasily died of massive organ failure, Lyudmilla says that there was not even a whole body to dress and bury. She says he was nothing but wounds.

The Soviet authorities buried Vasily in a plastic bag in a zinc-lined coffin in a separate, special cemetery because he was still radioactive enough to contaminate other people. But that was not the end of Lyudmilla's ordeal. When Vasily was first injured, she was six months pregnant. Two months after Vasily died, Lyudmilla gave birth to a baby girl who lived only four hours. The baby, exposed in her mother's womb to radiation from her father's body, had a damaged heart and liver. Children and fetuses are much more vulnerable to radiation damage than are adults because they are rapidly growing. This means their cells are rapidly dividing and easily affected by radioac-

The mother of Vasily Ignatenko mourns over his grave. Ignatenko absorbed a lethal dose of radiation after fighting the fire at Chernobyl. His body was so radioactive that he had to be buried in a zinc-lined coffin.

Survivor Guilt

Survivor guilt is the experience of feeling guilty for living through a disaster or trauma when others died. Seiko Fujimoto, who survived the Hiroshima, Japan, bombing during World War II when she was three years old, says it is a feeling that never goes away. Seiko and her baby brother lived with an aunt and uncle in Hiroshima. Both her aunt and uncle died immediately in the bombing. The body of their son, Seiko's cousin, was never found. Seiko herself survived radiation sickness to grow up, marry, and have children, but her brother died of radiation-caused cancer four years after the attack. He was five years old. Seiko never stopped suffering over the unfairness of her brother losing his life while she survived. She explains, "My brother never had a chance to grow up. I have two beautiful children and grandchildren. My brother never had a chance to enjoy . . . his nephew and grandnephew." Many radiation disaster survivors suffer similar guilt feelings about being able to live full lives when other people's lives were cut short.

Quoted in J.K. Yamamoto. "Survivors Speak Out at Hiroshima Commemoration." NikkeiWest, 2011. www.nikkeiwest.com/index.php/the-news/archived-article-list/138-survivors-speak-out-at-hiroshima-commemoration.

tive exposure. Lyudmilla lost two loved ones to the Chernobyl disaster. She mourned, "I killed her. . . . My little girl saved me, she took the whole radioactive shock into herself. She was like a lightning rod for it."[25] The mother had never truly grasped the peril of radiation for herself and the unborn baby.

Chernobyl's Damaged Heroes

Lyudmilla bravely tells her story, despite the pain that her memories cause her, because she wants the world to understand how a nuclear accident can damage lives. Other Chernobyl survivors are heroic because of the way they faced danger in order to save others. During the disaster, thousands of firefighters, soldiers, scientists, and other workers were sent to the site to put out the fires, bury the nuclear reactor in a sarcophagus, or coffin, of concrete and steel, and decontaminate the environment. These people were known as "liquidators" and were seen by their society as heroes for risking their lives. Their actions protected the

Builders who constructed the sarcophagus around the damaged reactor at Chernobyl hold a staff meeting next to the uncompleted structure in 1986. Thousands of firefighters, soldiers, scientists, and others risked or gave their lives to prevent further radioactive contamination of the environment.

larger society from potential widespread radiation exposure and an even worse disaster. Most were not exposed to enough radiation to develop ARS, but those who hurried to the site in the earliest days of the disaster were exposed to the most radiation, and some did suffer with radiation sickness. Konstantin Faschevsky, a staff member at the power plant, was one of those people. Unlike Vasily Ignatenko, he knew the danger when he raced to the plant in the hours after the explosions. He remembers, "I went to work understanding perfectly well I could die. . . . But I'm proud of myself and my colleagues for what we did."[26] Faschevsky and his colleagues were the ones who flooded the other reactors at the plant with water to cool them down and prevent further explosions and the release of more radiation.

Faschevsky remained at the crippled power plant for about a week before he began having symptoms of radiation sickness. He began experiencing nausea, vomiting, and headaches, but his ARS was mild, and he recovered without medical treatment after a two-week break from his work. Then he returned to Chernobyl to help the liquidators clean up the plant. He remained there for seven months, until he once again became ill. This time the radiation sickness was worse, and he was hospitalized for a month before he recovered.

In 2012 Faschevsky was fifty-seven years old and apparently healthy. He has never regretted doing his part at Chernobyl, but other liquidators suffered psychological and emotional problems for many years after the disaster. In one study of sixteen hundred liquidators conducted in 1993, a Russian clinic reported that 80 percent of the liquidators "were suffering from serious psychological problems,"[27] such as depression, memory problems, inability to concentrate, or serious mental illnesses such as schizophrenia. No one is sure whether these problems are caused by brain injury from radiation exposure or by emotional distress and trauma.

Lifelong Fears and Consequences

One of the emotional problems that people face after recovering from radiation sickness is fear for the future. People who have been exposed to acute, high levels of radiation may suffer long-term health effects—not from the radiation sickness itself but because of the damage that may be done to body cells by the exposure. These health effects may include cancers, premature aging, fatigue, and increased vulnerability to diseases. In addition, radiation sickness can leave permanent effects such as disfigured skin from burns or damaged eyes that require cataract removal surgeries. According to a few Russian medical studies, up to 90 percent of the Chernobyl liquidators—including those with chronic long-term radiation exposure, as well as those with acute exposures—are now invalids, suffering a variety of illnesses and unable to work or live independently. Once they have experienced radiation sickness, people cannot help but wonder what will come next.

One of the most common fears faced by survivors is about the genetic damage radiation can cause. Victims may worry that they will never be able to have children or that they are at risk of giving birth to children with genetic mutations and disabilities. The people of Chernobyl and the victims of the atom bombs dropped on Japan in 1945 have all experienced living with these fears. One woman, Katya, was a child in Pripyat at the time of the power plant disaster at Chernobyl. She was one of the children who rode their bikes toward the plant to see the fire. No one told them the danger they faced. Although exposed to high radiation levels, Katya survived and was evacuated with her family to another town. When she grew up, however, she was hesitant to get married. When asked why, she said, "I'm afraid. I'm afraid to love." She worried about what could happen if she had children and once said to an interviewer, "Do you know that it can be a sin to give birth?"[28] She and many other Chernobyl survivors feared having children who are damaged by radiation and have no chance of a normal life.

In Hiroshima and Nagasaki, Japan, many thousands of radiation victims risked marrying and having children and then worried about what would happen to the children. The Hiroshima bomb killed about 140,000 people, either from the initial blast or in the days following from radiation sickness. The Nagasaki bomb killed an estimated 70,000. According to the peace orga-

A memorial to the victims of the Chernobyl disaster in Kiev, Ukraine. According to studies, up to 90 percent of the surviving Chernobyl responders are now invalids from the effects of radiation.

nization International Campaign to Abolish Nuclear Weapons, some 270,000 "Hibakusha," or bomb-affected people, still live in Japan today. Thousands of these people survived radiation sickness. One of them is Tsunematsu Tanaka. In August 1945, when the first bomb was dropped, he was a married father of two who worked in Hiroshima. Tanaka survived the initial blast, but after about three weeks, he began to experience symptoms of radiation sickness. He had a fever, stomach pains, bloody diarrhea, and fatigue. In those days doctors did not know about radiation sickness, so Tanaka was diagnosed with an infectious disease, dysentery. Despite the misdiagnosis, he recovered because his ARS was mild. As time passed, Tanaka and the Japanese people learned about the destructive power of radiation, and Tanaka experienced other health effects from his exposure. For him, however, the worst effect was fear for his daughter, born in 1947. He worried that his radiation exposure had damaged her. He says, "I worried if she'd be affected by the A-bombing [atomic bombing]. There were times when I'd see her with a nosebleed or with something different from other children her kindergarten age and jumped to the conclusion that it must have had something to do with the A-bombing."[29] The child remained healthy and unaffected, but for all his life, Tanaka worried for her.

According to the World Health Organization, no genetic damage has been proved in children conceived by people who were previously exposed to radiation in Chernobyl. John D. Zimbrick, a scientist with the Health Physics Society, says that no children born to atom bomb survivors have been affected, either. He explains, "No genetic effects have been detected in a large sample (nearly 80,000) of offspring. By this, we mean that there is no detectable radiation-related increase in congenital abnormalities [birth defects], mortality (including childhood cancers), chromosome aberrations, or mutations in biochemically identifiable genes."[30] Scientific evidence, however, has not reassured all radiation survivors. In addition to the stress caused by these uncertainties, many have also experienced social prejudice and other negative reactions as radiation survivors.

Dealing with Social Prejudice

Sueko Hada was a Hibakusha who kept her secret as a survivor of the Hiroshima bombing for many years. She explains, "Generally, I didn't want other people to know I was a Hiro-

A choir consisting of atomic bomb survivors from World War
II sings a grieving song at the peace memorial ceremony on
August 9, 2010. About 270,000 bomb-affected people still live
in Japan today.

shima orphan. It wasn't respectable to be an orphan. Also, a
lot of Japanese people believed that if you'd been exposed to
A-bomb radiation you had a contagious disease. I know many
other survivors who have concealed their past from friends
and neighbors."[31] Chong Sansok is a Korean man who was a

An Actress's Legacy

Midori Naka was a famous Japanese actress who happened to be visiting Hiroshima, Japan, when the atom bomb was dropped on August 6, 1945. Initially, she seemed to have escaped unhurt, but within a few hours, she was vomiting. She managed to get to a hospital in Tokyo, where a team of doctors, including the best Japanese radiation expert at the time, Matsuo Tsuzuki, tried to save her life. Naka had severe ARS and died on August 24, but her suffering was the first chance that medical doctors had ever had to learn about and study radiation poisoning. She was the first person ever to have her cause of death officially listed as "atom bomb disease" (radiation sickness). Because of her fame, the cause of death was widely publicized in Japan. People learned what the new disease was and what symptoms could occur. Medical authorities began to investigate and research the syndrome and understand how it developed. Many historians believe that the publicity helped to save Japanese lives because victims were no longer misdiagnosed. Before her death, Naka was also the first person to give a firsthand account of the Hiroshima bombing to the media.

teenager living in Hiroshima in 1945 and had similar problems when he returned to his home culture. He survived radiation sickness in Japan and then moved back to Korea a few years later. There he felt that he had to keep his Hiroshima experience a secret from everyone. He explains, "Korean people think of us A-bomb survivors as having scary-looking injured faces. And they think your kids'll look like that too."[32] In some societies people exposed to radiation could be treated as tainted, abnormal, and frightening for all their lives.

As in Japan and Korea, the people exposed to radiation from the Chernobyl disaster faced social prejudice, too. They were labeled as "Chernobylites." Nikolai Kalugin, whose daughter died from radiation exposure, says, "People look at you differently. They ask you: Was it scary? How did the station burn? What did you see? And, you know, can you have children? Did your wife leave you? At first, we were all turned into animals. The very word 'Chernobyl' is like a signal. Everyone turns their head to look. He's from there!"[33] Other families who were evacuated from the Chernobyl area report feeling as if they are a separate people—Chernobylites instead of Ukrainians or Belarussians. One woman, Nadezhda Vygovskaya, says that her family was treated as contaminated. Her fourth-grade son was feared by the other children in his new school. The children thought he was radioactive and gave him the cruel nickname of "Shiny."

Social prejudice can be long lasting. In Japan, even when the children of the Hibakusha were born normal and healthy, the parents tried to keep their status a secret because the larger society viewed the children of the survivors with suspicion, too. Toshiko Tanaka, who was six years old when she suffered burns and radiation sickness in the Hiroshima bombing, explains, "Many survivors held their experiences inside and did not talk about it. They feared if they did talk, it would only work against them. They feared prejudice might put a stop to their children's marriage plans. And they thought nobody except those who actually survived will understand them anyway."[34] Tanaka, for example, did not even talk about her experiences with her own children until she was in her seventies. She says she wanted to forget her experiences and wanted her children to have a normal life and not feel sad for her.

Lasting Legacies: Using the Suffering for the Good of the World

As the decades have passed, many Hiroshima and Nagasaki survivors have finally become open about their experiences, and the attitudes of Japanese society have changed. The Hibakusha who are alive today want to share their memories with future generations and are honored in Japan for their willingness to teach others about the horrors of nuclear war. Toshiko Tanaka, for example, now speaks publicly about being a Hiroshima survivor. She shares her story with students and young people in schools all over the world in order to spread her message of peace and to argue against nuclear weapons. She says, "I wish that we will be the last survivors of nuclear weapons. If this wish is shared with people all over the world, I believe that some day we can accomplish a nuclear free world."[35]

Other Hibakusha have given a different legacy to the world. After World War II ended, these people willingly became research subjects for scientists and medical doctors who wanted to understand the long-term effects of radiation exposure. The Japanese National Research Council and the U.S. Atomic Bomb Casualty Commission studied thousands of survivors with examinations every year or two for decades in order to learn about the symptoms and course of radiation sickness, the effects of radiation exposure over a lifetime, and the long-term health of babies born to radiation-exposed people. In 1975 Japan and the United States jointly established the Radiation Effects Research Foundation (RERF) in Hiroshima to continue this medical research. Thousands of Hibakusha and their children continue to volunteer for the examinations and research because they want to help the world understand the effects of radiation. Evan Douple, a research chief at RERF, says, "The wealth of knowledge the survivors gave is truly a gift to all of mankind."[36] Because of the Hibakusha's contribution to medical science, scientists today not only understand radiation sickness but also are better able to prepare for possible future radiation emergencies and to search for new treatment methods that may save lives.

CHAPTER FIVE

The Future of Radiation Sickness Treatment and Prevention

The Chernobyl disaster in 1986 was the last time that a nuclear accident caused widespread radiation sickness. The bombings of Japan in 1945 during World War II was the one and only time that nuclear power was used in an act of aggression. These terrible events are far in the past, but that does not mean that dangerous and destructive radiation episodes cannot happen again. Scientists and many other people believe that the threat of a future nuclear disaster is very real—perhaps caused by a nuclear power accident or a terrorist or extremist attack with nuclear materials. Concern about the possibility of widespread radiation sickness in such an event drives the research of scientists today. Some of these scientists are concentrating their efforts on ways to prevent nuclear events. Others are researching ways to minimize human damage and death from radiation exposure and to develop new treatment methods for radiation sickness. Because there are still many unanswered questions about the effects of radiation exposure and because cases of radiation sickness are so rare, the work can be slow and difficult. Scientists trying to research new treatments have few patients to study, while those working to prevent nuclear accidents may be hampered by governmental or corporate resistance to instituting safety measures with limited evidence that the efforts are necessary. A recent nuclear event, however, provided strong evidence that the prevention and treatment research is needed.

The Lesson of Fukushima Daiichi

On March 11, 2011, the Fukushima Daiichi nuclear power plant in Japan suffered a major accident. On that date Japan was hit by a powerful magnitude 9.0 earthquake. Earthquakes are common in Japan, and all its nuclear power plants were built to withstand such a dangerous event. As it was designed to do, the Fukushima power plant shut down automatically when the quake hit, and the plant was constructed so well that no important damage occurred to the buildings in the plant. However, the earthquake caused a large, destructive tsunami that the nuclear power plant was not built to handle. Ocean water from the tsunami caused electric power to fail at the plant and also flooded the backup generators that were supposed to provide emergency power. This meant that the nuclear reactors in some of the plant's eleven generators could not be bathed with water from the electric pumps. As a result, the fissioning atoms of the reactor fuel in the nuclear core of the reactors could not be cooled. With no way to remove the heat from the cores, the radioactive material could heat up so much that it could cause a meltdown (in which the core melts and radiation is released) or even a nuclear explosion. The water that was already in the system was radioactive, and without electricity there was no way to remove it, cool it down, and dispose of it safely. In addition, even the systems used to monitor radioactivity in the plant were disabled by the tsunami. This was a true nuclear emergency that could have caused a Chernobyl-like disaster.

The Japanese government declared a nuclear emergency and evacuated people living within 12.4 miles (20km) of the crippled power plant. Hundreds of plant workers, scientists, firefighters, and military personnel raced to the plant to prevent a nuclear disaster, restore cooling to the cores, and shut down the nuclear reactors. Then, as the responders worked to restore electrical power and cool down the reactors, built-up steam from the reactors caused an explosion that released radioactive material into the air. It was from the radioactive water, not the nuclear core, but it was still a dangerous amount of radioactive material in the form of caesium and radioactive iodine. Fortunately, the people living in the area close to the power plant had already been evacuated when the radioactive release occurred. The emergency workers, however, were exposed.

This photo shows the demolished building housing reactor number four at the Fukushima Daiichi Nuclear Power Station in Japan, damaged by a 2011 tsunami.

At Risk of Death

The courageous plant workers who stayed at the facility while all the others were evacuated came to be known as the Fukushima 50. The approximately two hundred men who took on this role got the title because they worked in shifts, around the clock, in groups of fifty. In the hours and days after the disaster, these men fought to clear away debris and rubble so that firefighters could get in to hose down the crippled reactors. They worked to restore electricity to the plant, to repair what could be repaired, to cool the nuclear fuel, and to control the radioactive meltdown and prevent further explosions that could put a large portion of their country at risk. They worked despite knowing that they were exposing themselves to high

A worker at the Fukushima plant is checked for radiation exposure. Many workers received unsafe doses of radiation but not enough to cause radiation sickness.

levels of radiation. The daughter of one worker reportedly said of her father, "He has accepted his fate. Much like a death sentence."[37] One scientist, David Richardson, estimated that the workers were receiving as much radiation every hour as a U.S. nuclear plant worker is exposed to "over an entire career."[38]

Despite worldwide fears, only 167 workers received radiation dosages above 100 millisieverts (mSv),with just 6 receiving dosages over 250 mSv. (A millisievert is one-thousandth of a Sievert, which equals 100 rem.) These dosage levels are considered unsafe, but a dosage level of 1,000 mSv is needed to cause radiation sickness. According to the World Nuclear Association, no cases of radiation sickness occurred in any of the Fukushima 50, although the long-term effects on the workers are not yet known. No dosage levels that are thought to cause any potential problems have been found in the people living around the plant, either, but the area surrounding the plant is still contaminated and unlivable because of radioactivity in the environment. The accident at Fukushima reminded the world that the safety of nuclear power can never be taken for granted and that a major radiation accident could threaten people anywhere. Because of Fukushima, governments and nuclear scientists in many countries have proposed plans to prevent nuclear disasters and to improve the safety of nuclear power plants.

Prevention Efforts for the Future

One important lesson learned from the Fukushima accident is to be prepared for the unexpected. Japanese prime minister Yoshi-hiko Noda warns the world not to believe in the "myth of safety" of nuclear power. He says Japan now recognizes that it needs "a thoroughly prepared contingency plan based on the premise of preparing for the unanticipated risks."[39] To accomplish this, the Japanese government established the Nuclear Regulation Authority (NRA) in September 2012 to oversee safety measures in all its nuclear power plants. The United States has had such an agency, the Nuclear Regulatory Commission (NRC), since 1975. Because of the Fukushima accident, the NRC has decided to require that all 104 U.S. nuclear power plants have backup diesel generators for emergency power and backup water pumps in place by 2016. In addition, the NRC has ordered that older power plants be retrofitted with redesigned vent stacks—the pipes that ventilate gases from the reactors. This step will prevent the kind of explosions that occurred at Fukushima. In France nuclear power plant regulators have similarly instituted one hundred new rules for improving plant safety. Other European countries commissioned tests of all nuclear power plants to be certain that they could withstand unexpected events. According to nuclear safety experts, Fukushima-type accidents can be prevented in the future with improved safety measures and regulations. Reassessments of safety, however, are still ongoing around the world, and no changes to existing power plants have yet been made.

To many people nuclear power can never be safe enough. On the one-year anniversary of the Fukushima accident, protestors around the world demonstrated for an end to the use of nuclear power. Antinuclear activists in Japan, Europe, and the United States, as well as in other countries, fight for a future in which the world no longer uses nuclear power for energy. A Japanese newspaper, *Mainichi Shimbun*, for example, argued, "The illusion of nuclear power safety has been torn out by the root. The Fukushima nuclear disaster that followed the great waves of 11 March last year made sure of that."[40] Despite these ideas, however, most people believe that it is extremely unlikely that nuclear power plants will be shut down. Ana Palacio, for example, is a former foreign minister and World Bank executive from Spain. She explains that the world's need for energy is too great for a nuclear-free world to become a reality, and as a result, she says, "expansion of nuclear energy is, and will continue to be, a fact."[41] Because nuclear energy is likely to remain a fact of life, medical researchers and governments want to be prepared if an event that could cause widespread radiation sickness ever threatens to become a reality. Noda, for example, worries not only about accidents but also about a terrorist attack on a power plant. He warns, "A man-caused

Nuclear power plants are very controversial. Many people worldwide protest the existence of nuclear facilities, believing they can never be safe enough.

act of sabotage will test our imaginations far more than any natural disaster."[42] Noda wants governments and scientists to imagine and plan for any possible radiation situation, whether from an accident or a deliberate attack.

Noda urges planning and safety measures to prevent nuclear events, but medical scientists plan for what to do if prevention fails. They are working to develop new and better treatments for radiation sickness. Researchers rarely have human acute radiation syndrome (ARS) victims to study, but they can study

Securing Nuclear Weapons

Since he took office in 2009, President Barack Obama has been working on a four-year plan to secure all nuclear materials throughout the world that could be used in weapons and to prevent these materials from being stolen or smuggled to terrorist groups or rogue nations. The president's goal is not yet achieved, but he and other world leaders have made significant progress. For example, in 2010 the United States helped the countries of Serbia and Ukraine get rid of all nuclear materials and uranium that could be used for making weapons. Other countries, such as South Africa, Belarus, and Kazakhstan, have pledged to remove those materials soon. Obama is also leading an effort to establish nuclear security centers of excellence that would ensure a country would train security experts and keep track of all its nuclear materials, even those in research laboratories. So far, China, India, Japan, and South Korea have agreed to establish these centers. The president also wants the United States to commit to helping all countries prevent the proliferation of weapons of mass destruction. If he succeeds, an intentional nuclear event may be much less likely to threaten people in the future.

U.S. president Barack Obama (left) and Russian president Dmitry Medvedev sign the New START nuclear arms reduction treaty on April 8, 2010.

the effects of radiation in animals and try to develop new treatments for them. They also can learn about the effects of radiation and how to treat symptoms with people who are undergoing radiation therapy for cancer.

Radiation Therapy and Radiation Sickness

Radiation therapy is the use of radiation to kill cells or prevent them from dividing and multiplying. Cancer is characterized by abnormal, defective body cells that divide and multiply without control. Therefore, killing or damaging these cells kills the cancer. The National Cancer Institute explains, "Radiation therapy uses high-energy radiation to shrink tumors and kill cancer cells. X-rays, gamma rays, and charged particles are types of radiation used for cancer treatment. The radiation may be delivered by a machine outside the body (external-beam radiation therapy), or it may come from radioactive material placed in the body near cancer cells (internal radiation therapy)."[43] This medical use of radiation is highly controlled and targeted to the cancer area, but it is not perfect. Normal body cells are damaged by the radiation treatment, too. This is why people can experience hair loss, skin reddening, nausea, and fatigue while undergoing radiation therapy. The radiation is damaging not only rapidly dividing cancer cells but also rapidly dividing cells of the intestinal tract, hair, skin, and bone marrow. Cancer patients receiving radiation therapy actually are experiencing very mild forms of radiation sickness. If these symptoms can be prevented or treated, then the symptoms of ARS might be treated and prevented in the same way.

Some people receiving radiation therapy develop low white blood cell counts, which weakens their immune systems so that they cannot fight infections. The biotechnology company Cellerant Therapeutics has developed a medical treatment to boost the immune systems for these people. The treatment is called CLT-008. The treatment involves the use of stem cells that can become red blood cells, platelets, and white blood cells in a person's body. Stem cells are the special cells in the body from which all other cells can be generated. In the bone marrow they are called hematopoietic stem cells or precursor cells. These hematopoietic stem cells can make more of themselves through the process of cell division and can differentiate or mature into all the kinds of blood cells that might need to be replaced. Researchers at Cellerant Therapeutic developed a method of growing these stem cells in the laboratory and then injecting them into patients suffering from weakened immune systems because of their cancer treatments. In 2011 the researchers began their first tests of this treatment in cancer patients.

Tests of new treatments for people are called clinical trials and usually occur in three phases that are regulated by the National Institutes of Health. All new treatments and medications

A technician prepares a patient for radiation therapy. Radiation is used to kill cancer cells or prevent them from multiplying.

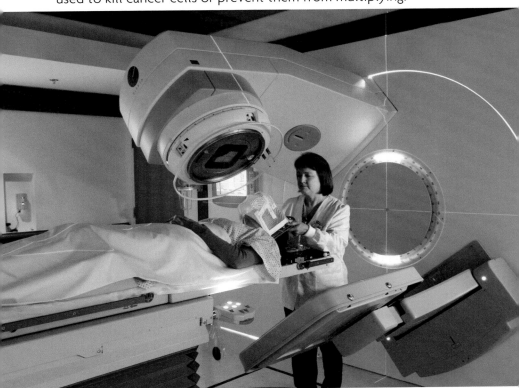

must receive approval through clinical trials before they are approved for general use by the U.S. Food and Drug Administration (FDA). When Cellerant Therapeutics conducted its first phase 1 safety trial with a small number of volunteer patients, the researchers discovered that the drug worked quite well to boost the immune system and caused no problems. The researchers conducted a larger phase 2 trial and got the same positive results. Perhaps, theorized the researchers, CLT-008 would work even in people exposed to higher levels of radiation. A whole bone marrow transplant would not be necessary, and with a treatment that uses only stem cells, no donors with a genetic match would be needed.

Will It Work for Radiation Sickness, Too?

The researchers could not test the treatment in people with severe radiation sickness because no scientist would expose a person to high radiation levels on purpose. Instead, they tested their treatment in animals that they exposed to increasing doses of radiation. Even when exposed to bacteria and fungi, the animals survived to recover from ARS with the CLT-008 treatment. Their immune systems were boosted with the treatment, and they successfully fought off infections. The researchers also discovered that CLT-008 worked in animals that did not receive treatment right away. The treatment worked when given to the test animals for up to five days after exposure. Ram Mandalam, the president of Cellerant Therapeutics, explained, "That's important in cases such as what's happening in Japan, where people may not learn the level [of radiation] they have been exposed to until 24 to 48 hours later."[44]

CLT-008 has another advantage: It can be developed in large quantities and stored in case it is needed for a widespread nuclear disaster in the future. It is the kind of treatment that the U.S. government wants available if a radiation emergency occurs. The government's Biomedical Advanced Research and Development Authority (BARDA) has developed a program called Project BioShield to procure and encourage development of medical approaches for radiation emergencies. This program gave Cellerant Therapeutics a five-year research grant and contract to test and develop CLT-008 for stockpiling in case it is ever needed. Cellerant Therapeutics hopes to be able to get FDA approval for the new treatment by 2016. To be approved as a treatment for ARS, CLT-008 will not be tested in human trials, as is usual for most medicines. The FDA has a special approval method—the Animal Efficacy Rule—that can be used, it says, "When Human Efficacy Studies Are Not Ethical or Feasible."[45] If CLT-008 proves to be effective in several species of animals and safe in healthy human volunteers, it will be approved for emergency use in a radiation disaster. BARDA will buy and keep it in the Strategic National Stockpile of emergency medicines.

Saving Body Organs from ARS

CLT-008 is not the only ARS stem cell treatment supported by BARDA. In 2008 two biotechnology companies, Osiris Therapeutics and Genzyme Corporation, were awarded a contract to work on another treatment for ARS that is named Prochymal. Prochymal is made from bone marrow cells called mesenchymal cells that are drawn from the bone marrow of healthy volunteers. The cells are then grown and multiplied in the laboratory and injected into the bloodstreams of people who have diseases that cause cell damage. Originally, Prochymal was developed as a treatment for people with diseases such as heart attacks, diabetes, or Crohn's disease (a disorder of the gastrointestinal tract). The stem cell treatment helps damaged organs grow new cells and heal. Prochymal is currently in phase 3 clinical trials with a large number of people who have some of these diseases, but the trials usually take several years before the medicine receives FDA approval. In the meantime, the researchers are also studying the use of Prochymal for ARS. They are testing the effectiveness of the treatment in animals and will use the Animal Efficacy Rule to get FDA approval. Thomas J. MacVittie, a scientist with the Strategic National Stockpile, explains, "Prochymal has demonstrated therapeutic utility in humans repairing many of the major organ systems

A technician cultivates stem cells in a laboratory. Stem cells may help radiation sickness patients regenerate new blood cells.

affected by radiation injury. Where most approaches only target a single component of ARS, Prochymal has the potential to address the entire syndrome including both acute and delayed effects in multiple organ systems."[46] If all goes well, Prochymal may be the first treatment for both bone marrow syndrome and gastrointestinal syndrome in radiation sickness. Doses of it could be stored by the thousands in the Strategic National Stockpile against future need.

Researching New Uses for Existing Drugs

Other medicines that could be stockpiled for the future are being studied by a research team at Children's Hospital Boston and the Dana-Farber Cancer Institute of Harvard University. The team is investigating two drugs that already have been approved by the FDA as safe and effective for people with other medical problems. The drugs are a powerful antibiotic

Preparing for an Emergency

The Centers for Disease Control and Prevention (CDC) recommends that everyone know what to do in the event of a nuclear emergency. On its website, the CDC explains that quick action can protect people and minimize their radiation exposure, whether it is from a nuclear power plant accident, a dirty bomb, or any other kind of release of nuclear materials. If a radiation event occurs, the CDC says:

- Get inside and stay inside an undamaged building.
- If possible, shower and change into clean clothes.
- Stay tuned to television or radio for updates and instructions.

Centers for Disease Control and Prevention. "Radiation Emergencies: Emergency Preparedness and Response." September 22, 2011. www.bt.cdc.gov/radiation/types ofemergencies.asp.

called fluoroquinolone and an infection-fighting protein called rBPI$_{21}$. The protein is a laboratory-made version of the natural infection-fighting protein in the body known as BPI. The researchers are testing this drug combination in mice. In the first studies, in 2011 the scientists exposed the mice to 7 gray of radiation. This dose would normally be fatal to the mice 95 percent of the time. Twenty-four hours after the radiation exposure, the scientists began treating some of the mice every day with doses of fluoroquinolone. Others got daily doses of rBPI$_{21}$. Another group received a combination of both drugs every day. The mice that got the combined treatment began growing new white blood cells to fight infections. After thirty days, 80 percent of the mice that were treated with rBPI$_{21}$ and fluoroquinolone were still alive and healthy. The researchers have much more work to do before they are sure that they have found an effective treatment for ARS. However, says Ofer

Levy, a lead scientist in the study, "both fluoroquinolone anti-biotics and rBPI$_{21}$ have been shown to be quite safe in humans. Their combined effectiveness in our study involving mice is an indication that they may be equally beneficial in people."[47]

To Conquer Radiation Sickness

The scientific team at Harvard is just one of the many groups of researchers around the world who take the need for ARS treatment very seriously. Eva Guinan, another lead scientist in the Harvard research, explains, "There is great interest in creating systems for dealing with the short- and long-term health risks of a significant release of radiation, whether from an accident at a nuclear power plant, an act of terrorism, or even a small-scale incident in which a CT machine [a computerized tomography medical scanner that uses nuclear material] malfunctions."[48] Today's medical and radiation scientists are working toward the discovery of treatment methods that can stop or reverse radiation sickness and prevent ARS from killing its victims. The U.S. government with Project BioShield and the Strategic National Stockpile has the same goal. Even if effective treatments for radiation sickness are never needed on a large scale, scientists and government experts are determined to be ready and save lives if the worst occurs.

Notes

Introduction: The Relevance of Radiation Sickness Today

1. Amit Bhasin and Aparna Ahuja. "Harnessing Nuclear Energy: Health Risks." *Indian Journal of Medical Specialties*, January–June 2011, p. 46. www.ijms.in/articles/2/1/Harnessing-Nuclear-Energy.html.
2. Quoted in *NOVA*. "Preparing for Nuclear Terrorism." Interview Graham Allison. PBS, February 25, 2003. www.pbs.org/wgbh/nova/military/preparing-for-nuclear-terrorism.html.

Chapter One: What Is Radiation?

3. Health Physics Society. "Types of Radiation." Radiation Answers. www.radiationanswers.org/radiation-introduction/types-of-radiation.html.
4. Health Physics Society. "Ionizing Radiation." Radiation Answers. www.radiationanswers.org/radiation-introduction/types-of-radiation/ionizing-radiation.html.
5. U.S. Nuclear Regulatory Commission. "Radiation Basics." December 6, 2011. www.nrc.gov/about-nrc/radiation/health-effects/radiation-basics.html#ionizing.
6. Health Physics Society. "Radiation Exposure." Radiation Answers. www.radiationanswers.org/radiation-introduction/radiation-exposure.html.
7. International Atomic Energy Agency. "Factsheets & FAQS: Radiation in Everyday Life." www.iaea.org/Publications/Factsheets/English/radlife.html.

Chapter Two: What Is Radiation Sickness?

8. Centers for Disease Control and Prevention. "Acute Radiation Syndrome: A Fact Sheet for Physicians." March 18, 2005. www.bt.cdc.gov/radiation/arsphysicianfactsheet.asp.

9. Arnold S. Dion. "Acute Radiation Sickness." Harry K. Daghlian Jr.: America's First Peacetime Atom Bomb Fatality. http://members.tripod.com/~Arnold_Dion/Daghlian/sickness.html.

10. Thomson Reuters Integrity. *Disease Briefing: Acute Radiation Syndrome.* Thomson Reuters. http://thomson reuters.com/content/science/pdf/ls/radiation_briefing.pdf.

11. Quoted in Martin Zeilig. "Louis Slotin and the Invisible Killer: A Young Canadian Scientist Gave His Life to Save His Friends When an Experiment Went Wrong." *Beaver*, August/September 1995. Atomic Heritage Foundation. www.atomicheritage.org/index.php?id=92&option=com _content&task=view.

12. Centers for Disease Control and Prevention. "Acute Radiation Syndrome."

13. Centers for Disease Control and Prevention. "Acute Radiation Syndrome."

Chapter Three: Treatment of Radiation Sickness

14. Mayo Clinic Staff. "Treatments and Drugs: Radiation Sickness." Mayo Clinic, March 17, 2011. www.mayoclinic.com /health/radiation-sickness/DS00432/DSECTION=treatments -and-drugs.

15. Mayo Clinic Staff. "Treatments and Drugs."

16. Jerrold T. Bushberg. "Radiation Exposure and Contamination." *The Merck Manual*, June 2009. www.merckmanuals .com/professional/injuries_poisoning/radiation_exposure _and_contamination/radiation_exposure_and_contamin ation.html.

17. Quoted in Annette Cary. "Atomic Man Still Has Lessons to Teach After 35 Years." *Tri-City Herald* (Kennewick, WA), September 14, 2011. http://m.spokesman.com/stories/2011 /sep/14/atomic-man-still-has-lessons-teach-after-35-years.

18. International Atomic Energy Agency. *The Radiological Accident in Goiânia.* Vienna: International Atomic Energy Association, 1988. www-pub.iaea.org/MTCD/publications /PDF/Pub815_web.pdf.

19. A.E. Baranov. "Transplantation of Bone Marrow in Victims of the Chernobyl Accident." International Atomic Energy

Agency, June 30, 2011. www.iaea.org/INIS/search/Chernobyl /Key_documents/20075993.html.

20. Mayo Clinic Staff. "Treatments and Drugs."

21. Jamie K. Waselenko et al. "Medical Management of the Acute Radiation Syndrome: Recommendations of the Strategic National Stockpile Radiation Group." *Annals of Internal Medicine*, June 15, 2004, p. 1047. www.annals .org/content/140/12/1037.full.pdf+html.

Chapter Four: Life After Radiation Sickness

22. Quoted in Svetlana Alexievich. *Voices from Chernobyl: The Oral History of a Nuclear Disaster.* Translated by Keith Gessen. New York: Picador, 2006, pp. 5–6.

23. Quoted in Alexievich. *Voices from Chernobyl*, p. 11.

24. Quoted in Alexievich. *Voices from Chernobyl*, p. 17.

25. Quoted in Alexievich. *Voices from Chernobyl*, p. 22.

26. Quoted in Tony Halpin. "I Battled Chernobyl Radiation, Says N-Plant Worker." *Australian* (Surry Hills, New South Wales), March 24, 2011. www.theaustralian.com.au/news /world/i-battled-chernobyl-radiation-says-n-plant-worker /story-e6frg6so-1226027019879.

27. Sebastian Pflugbeil et al. *Health Effects of Chernobyl: 25 Years After the Reactor Catastrophe.* Berlin: Strahlen-telex, German Affiliate of International Physicians for the Prevention of Nuclear War, April 2011, p. 23. www.ratical .org/radiation/Chernobyl/HEofC25yrsAC.html#02.04.

28. Quoted in Alexievich. *Voices from Chernobyl*, pp. 104–105.

29. Tsunematsu Tanaka. "My Experiences of the A-bombing." National Peace Memorial Halls for the Atomic Bomb Victims in Hiroshima and Nagasaki. www.global-peace.go.jp /en/taikenki/detail_09_2.html.

30. John D. Zimbrick. "Answer to Question #340 Submitted to 'Ask the Experts.'" Health Physics Society, July 28, 2000. http://hps.org/publicinformation/ate/q340.html.

31. Quoted in Patrick Cox and Jennifer Goren. "Hiroshima's Survivors." Transcript. *The World*, Public Radio International, 2006. Dart Center for Journalism & Trauma. http://dart center.org/content/hiroshimas-survivors.

32. Quoted in Cox and Goren. "Hiroshima's Survivors."

33. Quoted in Alexievich. *Voices from Chernobyl*, p. 31.

34. Toshiko Tanaka. "Meet Toshiko Tanaka: My Experience of the Atomic Bomb in Hiroshima." Hibakusha Stories. www.hibakushastories.org/toshiko-tanaka.html.
35. Tanaka. "Meet Toshiko Tanaka.
36. Quoted in Jennifer Walsh. "After the Fallout: Study on Atomic Bomb Survivors Marks 60 Years." *In Focus*, Winter/Spring 2008, p. 16. www.infocusmagazine.org /portable/8.1.pdf.

Chapter Five: The Future of Radiation Sickness Treatment and Prevention

37. Quoted in Molly Hennessy-Fiske. "Who Are the Fukushima 50?" *Los Angeles Times*, March 17, 2011. http://articles.la times.com/2011/mar/17/world/la-fgw-japan-quake-fukushima -50.
38. Quoted in Paul Harper. "Heroes of Fukushima—50 Remain at Daiichi." *New Zealand Herald* (Auckland), March 16, 2011. www.nzherald.co.nz/japan-tsunami/news/article .cfm?c_id=1503051&objectid=10712802.
39. Quoted in UPI. "Japan: Lessons Learned from Fukushima." UPI.com, March 28, 2012. www.upi.com/Business_News /Energy-Resources/2012/03/28/Japan-Lessons-learned-from -Fukushima/UPI-63821332949624.
40. Quoted in Justin McCurry. "How Fukushima Is Leading Towards a Nuclear-Free Japan." *Guardian* (London), March 9, 2012. www.guardian.co.uk/environment/2012/mar /09/fukushima-reactors-nuclear-free-japan.
41. Ana Palacio. "Fukushima, Europe's Nuclear Test." Aljazeera, March 14, 2012. www.aljazeera.com/indepth /opinion/2012/03/2012311142820723699.html.
42. Quoted in UPI. "Japan."
43. National Cancer Institute. "Radiation Therapy for Cancer." June 30, 2010. www.cancer.gov/cancertopics/fact sheet/Therapy/radiation.
44. Quoted in Jeremy Hsu. "New Treatment May Prevent Deadly Radiation Sickness." Innovation News Daily, March 23, 2011. www.innovationnewsdaily.com/143 -nuclear-radiation-sickness-treatment.html.
45. U.S. Food and Drug Administration. "New Drug and Biological Drug Products; Evidence Needed to Demonstrate

Effectiveness of New Drugs When Human Efficacy Studies Are Not Ethical or Feasible." *Federal Register* (Washington, DC), May 31, 2002. www.fda.gov/ohrms /dockets/98fr/053102a.htm.

46. Quoted in Osiris Therapeutics. "Osiris Therapeutics Awarded Department of Defense Contract for Prochymal™ Fully Valued at $224.7 Million." January 3, 2008.http://inves tor.osiris.com/releasedetail.cfm?releaseid=284617.

47. Quoted in Robert Levy. "Alleviating Radiation Sickness." *Harvard University Gazette*, November 23, 2011. http://news .harvard.edu/gazette/story/2011/11/alleviating-radiation -sickness.

48. Quoted in Levy. "Alleviating Radiation Sickness."

Glossary

acute: Occurring in a brief length of time and in an intense amount.

alpha particle: One of the types of radiation emitted by radioactive material. Alpha particles are positively charged and consist of two protons and two neutrons.

beta particle: One of the types of radiation emitted by radioactive substances. A beta particle is a high-speed electron.

bone marrow: The soft tissue in the center of bones that contains the cells that produce red blood cells, white blood cells, platelets, and bone-forming cells.

cataract: Cloudiness on the normally clear lens of the eye that can interfere with vision.

chronic: Persisting for a long time.

decontamination: The process of freeing a person from a contaminating substance such as radiation particles.

deoxyribonucleic acid (DNA): The chemicals that carry the coding instructions for body structures and functions. DNA is found in the nucleus of each cell in the body.

dosimeter badge: A device worn by radiation workers that measures and records radiation exposure.

electron: A fundamental particle of the atom that carries a negative electrical charge and orbits the atom's nucleus.

element: Scientifically, an element is a substance that cannot be broken down into simpler substances by chemical means. Each atom of an element has the same number of protons as all the other atoms of that element. There are 117 known elements; 92 of them are found in nature, and the rest are human made.

fission: The splitting of an unstable atom's nucleus into two or more nuclei. Nuclear fission releases high amounts of energy and radioactivity.

gamma ray: The high-energy penetrating radiation that can be emitted during nuclear decay or nuclear reactions.

gastrointestinal tract: The stomach and intestines.

hemorrhage: A condition of abnormal, hard-to-control bleeding from the blood vessels.

immune system: The complex system in the body that fights disease and the invasion of foreign material.

ion: An electrically charged atom that has lost or gained one or more electrons and is therefore no longer balanced because the number of electrons is different from the number of protons in the atom.

ionizing radiation: High-energy radiation in the form of particles or rays that is capable of ionizing the atoms through which it passes.

isotope: Any of the two or more forms of an element with the same number of protons in the nucleus but different numbers of neutrons. A radioactive isotope has an unstable nucleus and emits radiation in order to become stable.

lymphocyte: A small white blood cell that is a part of the immune system and helps protect the body against disease.

neutron: The subatomic particle in the nucleus of an atom that carries no charge. The number of neutrons in the atom determines its isotope.

neutron radiation: A highly penetrating type of radiation in which neutrons are ejected from the nucleus of the atom.

nucleus: The center of the atom. It consists of protons and neutrons and is positively charged.

proton: The subatomic particle in the nucleus of the atom that is positively charged. The number of protons in the atom determines the element.

radioactive decay: The disintegration of the nucleus of an unstable atom, during which radioactive particles are emitted until the atom becomes stable.

stem cell: The master cell in the human body that has no specific function but can differentiate, or grow into, any one of the body's more than two hundred specific cells. Stem cells enable the body to renew and repair itself. Stem cells are found in many organs of the body.

transfusion: The process of transferring whole blood or components of blood from one person (the donor) to another (the recipient) through a needle inserted into a vein.

Organizations to Contact

Centers for Disease Control and Prevention (CDC)

1600 Clifton Rd.
Atlanta, GA 30333
Phone: (800) 232-4636
Website: www.cdc.gov

The CDC provides extensive emergency management and preparedness information for radiation events, including general information about radiation exposure and how individuals and families can protect themselves.

Hiroshima Peace Memorial Museum

1-2 Nakajimama-cho, Naka-ku
Hiroshima City 730-0811, Japan
Phone: +81-82-241-4004
Website: www.pcf.city.hiroshima.jp/top_e.html

The Hiroshima Peace Memorial Museum is devoted to the memory of the people who suffered the atomic bombings in Hiroshima and Nagasaki. People can visit the museum in Japan or visit a virtual museum online with educational information, photographic exhibits, survivor stories, and declarations for peace in the world.

International Atomic Energy Agency (IAEA)

IAEA Office at the United Nations
1 United Nations Plaza, Rm. DC-1-1155
New York, NY 10017
Phone: (212) 963-6010
Website: www.iaea.org

The IAEA works for international cooperation with nuclear materials and decisions and promotes the peaceful use of nuclear power. In an emergency such as a nuclear power plant accident, it sends a mission of experts to help assess and control the situation and to provide continually updated information to the public about the crisis.

Oak Ridge Institute for Science and Education (ORISE)

PO Box 117
Oak Ridge, TN 37831
Phone: (865) 576-3146
Website: http://orise.orau.gov/default.aspx

Under the auspices of the U.S. Department of Energy, the ORISE mission includes nuclear research and development, protecting the public and the environment, and ensuring national readiness in case of a nuclear emergency. It maintains a complete database of radiation accidents worldwide, along with assessments of why they occurred and how they could have been prevented, and it provides emergency medical response teams for radiation incidents anywhere in the world. The ORISE is also committed to public education about nuclear research, health, and safety.

U.S. Food and Drug Administration (FDA)

10903 New Hampshire Ave.
Silver Spring, MD 20993
Phone: (800) 463-6332
Website: www.fda.gov

The FDA is charged with protecting and ensuring the public health. It is responsible for approving medicinal drugs, guarding the food supply, and assessing products that emit radiation, such as medical devices, microwaves, and cell phones. It offers educational information for the public about the safety and usage of devices that emit radiation, as well as general information about radiation dosages and health.

For More Information

Books

Arthur Gillard, ed. *Nuclear Power*. Farmington Hills, MI: Greenhaven, 2011. This book explores the political, moral, and social issues of nuclear power from the perspectives of different authors.

Sue Vander Hook. *The Manhattan Project*. Minneapolis: Essential Library/ABDO, 2011. The author describes the secret World War II project that led to the development of the first atomic bombs and the beginning of the nuclear age.

P. Andrew Karam and Ben P. Stein. *Radioactivity*. New York: Chelsea House, 2009. This general overview explains what radiation is, where it comes from, how it can affect humans, and how radiation can be both useful and destructive.

Jill Karson. *Nuclear Power*. San Diego: ReferencePoint, 2010. This book examines the use of nuclear power for energy in the United States, whether it is safe, how it affects the environment, and what the future of nuclear power might be.

Marcia Amidon Lusted. *The Chernobyl Disaster*. Minneapolis: Essential Library/ABDO, 2011. This book explains, describes, and explores the details of the nuclear power plant accident at Chernobyl. The author also discusses the long-term effects of the disaster on people and the environment.

Websites

Chernobyl Journal, Timm Suess.com (http://timmsuess.com /chernobyl-journal). In 2009 the photographer Tim Suess made a trip to the evacuated, abandoned areas around the destroyed Chernobyl nuclear power plant. He offers his pictures as documentation of the still radioactive so-called zone of exclusion, the land that remains uninhabitable.

National Peace Memorial Halls for the Atomic Bomb Victims in Hiroshima and Nagasaki (www.global-peace .go.jp/en/index.php). At this site, visitors can read, watch, and listen to many testimonies and stories from atomic bomb survivors.

Nuclear Science and Technology, American Nuclear Society (www.aboutnuclear.org/home.cgi). At this information website for students, visitors will find detailed explanations of the use of nuclear science in the areas of food irradiation, industry, medicine, space, and energy.

Physics 2000, University of Colorado at Boulder (www .colorado.edu/physics/2000/cover.html). Explore the world of physics, atoms, and radioactivity at this interactive website. Use the Table of Contents, for example, to find "Isotopes and Radioactivity." Then click on "Halflife" to watch radioactive decay in action.

10 Famous Incidents of Death by Radiation, Listverse (http://listverse.com/2010/03/25/10-famous-incidences-of-death-by-radiation). This is one person's list of the ten most interesting and well-known deaths from radiation throughout history. Each event is described with a photo and a short description of what happened.

Index

Picture Credits

About the Author

Toney Allman holds a bachelor of science degree from Ohio State University and a master's degree from the University of Hawaii. She currently lives in Virginia and has written more than forty nonfiction books for students on a variety of medical and scientific topics.